ADVANCE PRAISE FOR

The Salmon Shanties

"Rhenisch's words sing as water moves through them, making us one with the sea. Just as salmon deliver old bones in new dresses, these poems refresh the songs of innocence. As the spawning streams labour, they sing out lyrics from this poet of the land." —LINDA ROGERS

"The land and waters themselves entrusted Harold Rhenisch to write these transcendent poems." —KATHLEEN FLENNIKEN, poet of *Plume* and former Washington Poet Laureate

"This is an astonishing book. It rips the world open. It takes no prisoners. It upends the entire overlay of globalism that has turned a peach into an industrial product. It is an ecstatic unravelling of the delusions of the present. Rhenisch's visionary and prophetic voice joins those of the Indigenous Cascadian past to restore, in poetry, the sane and beautiful way of its waterkeepers." —SHARON THESEN

"Immersed in *The Salmon Shanties,* I feel like I've been following spawning kokanee all the way to the mountains, guided by the songs of sandhill cranes. These are the most expansive—at once loamy and riparian, documentary and cosmic—and the most learned, and the most rhythmically musical poems I've read in a long time (possibly ever). Using the pruning tools of language, Harold Rhenisch has plotted a four-dimensional map of Cascadia—for many of us, it's a map home—and I'm grateful. For decades Harold Rhenisch has walked, mapped, and dreamed Cascadia. These are his songs. But Harold would probably be the first to say he didn't write these shanties; he's simply the one who listened and wrote them down. These are words for watching the first salmon swim back to the mountains. Chants against the wasters of water, against the builders

of industrial apple plantations. These are songs for the sandhill cranes, who stitch the world together in the oldest of stories."
—KELLY SHEPHERD, author of *Dog and Moon*

"Rhenisch's poems weave geography, ecology, and metaphor in unexpected ways. His writing is full of energy and insight."
—DON GAYTON, ecologist and author of *The Sky and the Patio: An Ecology of Home*

"Harold is a magical 'singer of this land,' calling us home, to our Illahie, where we belong. Bursting with energies, these songs of Cascadia pour through like a waterfall cascading over the edge of history. When you begin to listen deeply, the land may begin to dream through you. Harold here becomes the bard or senachie of Cascadia.

A book about Totem Salmon coming home, a path we should follow. It's about 'living in a country without borders.' Here we finally begin to come to terms with the life of this place, what we have done and lost, especially with the First Peoples here, and what the place requires of us. These 'shanties' are chanted sing-song incantations to save our lives, to bring back the Land and 'The-Spirit-in-the Land.' In incantatory lamentations, Harold sings: 'Let me stay with the Earth until she has done weeping.' It's a great story of transformation of we, the people, in this land, in coming home. A remarkable achievement creating this song-cycle of 'mythic' yet real scope and depth. Nobody tells this story like Harold Rhenisch, a real breakthrough in bioregional poetry-and-history. An eloquent elegy evoking the story of the place and its people."
—DAVID MCCLOSKEY, Cascadia Institute

OSKANA POETRY & POETICS

Harold Rhenisch

The Salmon Shanties

A CASCADIAN SONG CYCLE

University of Regina Press

Printed and bound in Canada at Imprimerie Gauvin. The text of this book is printed on 100% post-consumer recycled paper with earth-friendly vegetable-based inks.

Cover art: "Fish wave black seamless pattern" (modified) by VETOCHKA / Adobe Stock and "Salmon fillet texture, fish pattern" (modified) by biancaoddi / Adobe Stock

Cover and text design: Duncan Campbell, University of Regina Press

Series Editor: Randy Lundy
Managing Editor: Shannon Parr
Copy Editor: Crissy Calhoun
Proofreader: Kelly Laycock

The text and titling faces are Arno, designed by Robert Slimbach.

Canada Council for the Arts Conseil des arts du Canada

Canada

creative SASKATCHEWAN

Library and Archives Canada Cataloguing in Publication

Title: The salmon shanties : a cascading song cycle / Harold Rhenisch.

Other titles: Cascading song cycle

Names: Rhenisch, Harold, 1958- author.

Description: Poems. | Includes glossary of chinook wawa.

Identifiers: Canadiana (print) 20240363310 | Canadiana (ebook) 20240363329 | ISBN 9781779400154 (softcover) | ISBN 9781779400178 (EPUB) | ISBN 9781779400161 (PDF)

Subjects: LCGFT: Poetry.

Classification: LCC PS8585.H54 S25 2024 | DDC C811/.54—dc23

10 9 8 7 6 5 4 3 2

UNIVERSITY OF REGINA PRESS
University of Regina
Regina, Saskatchewan
Canada S4S 0A2
TELEPHONE: (306) 585-4758
FAX: (306) 585-4699
WEB: www.uofrpress.ca
EMAIL: uofrpress@uregina.ca

We acknowledge the support of the Canada Council for the Arts for our publishing program. We acknowledge the financial support of the Government of Canada. / Nous reconnaissons l'appui financier du gouvernement du Canada. This publication was made possible with support from Creative Saskatchewan's Book Publishing Production Grant Program.

In memoriam: Ezra Pound & Charles Lillard

Shantie*: to sing; a song*

—From Chinook Wawa,
the language of the Columbia District

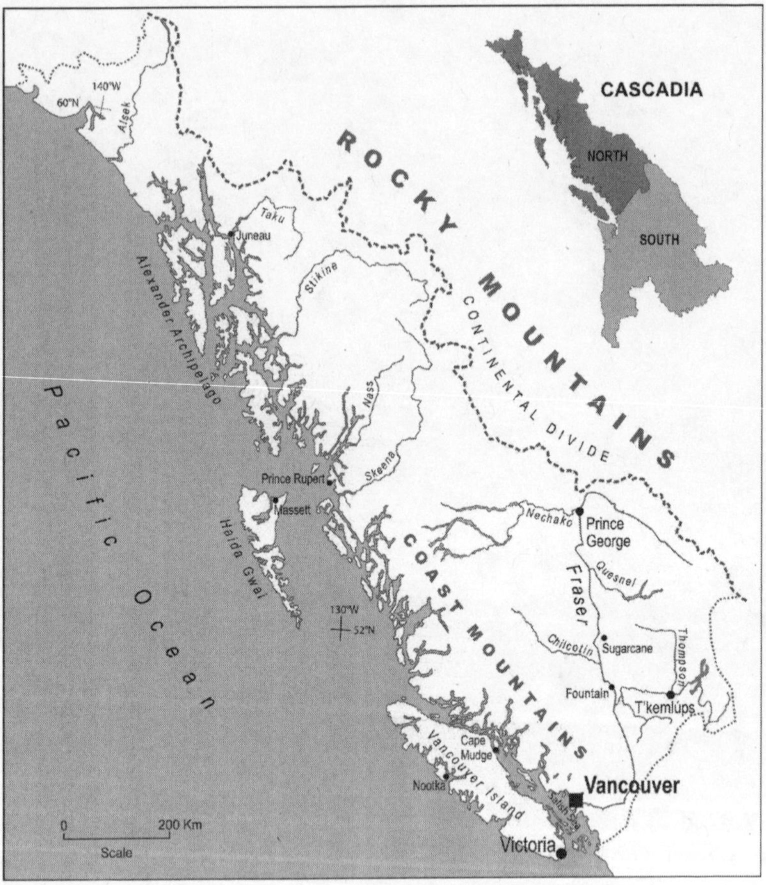

Maps adapted by Trista Bassett and Harold Rhenisch from David McCloskey's "Map of Cascadia" (2015), Cascadia.Institute.org with permission.

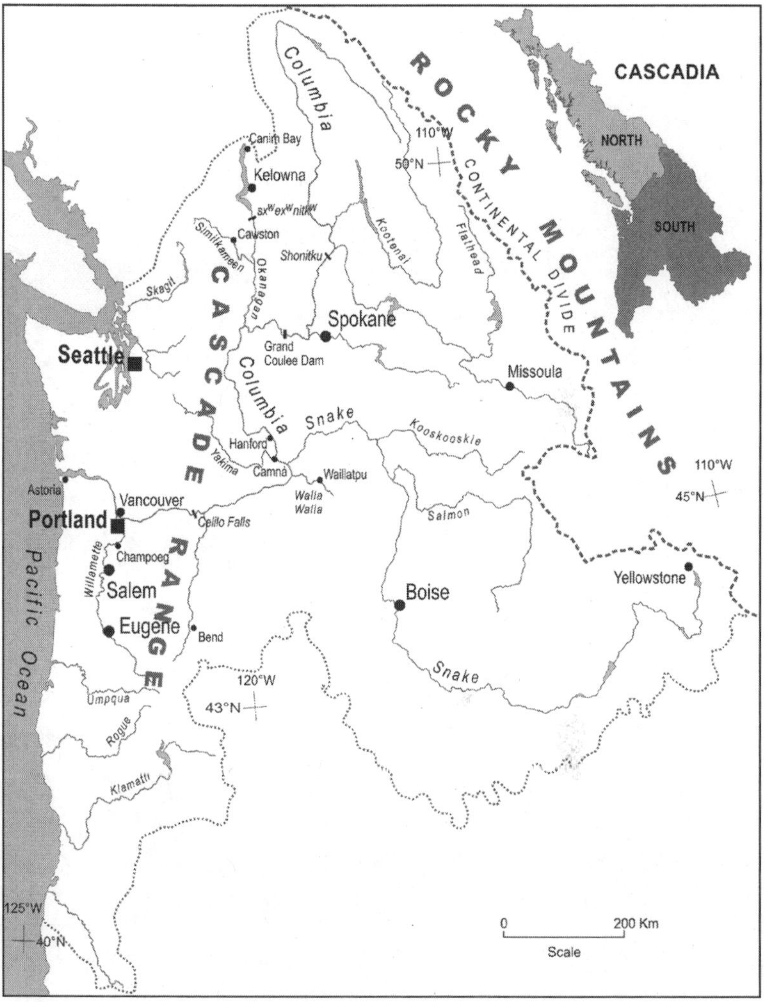

The second edition of McCloskey's large map "Cascadia: A Great Green Land" (2023) is available from FeatheredStarProductions.com. Adapted here with permission.

CONTENTS

BONE SONG

an invocation

There is no need now to be shy. The scarlet beetles sure aren't.
They join among bees grazing on the pink pillows of the wavy thistles

that still catch the wind here and there in the salsify,
looking up dreamily, drenched in golden pollen, and so, by loving,

they keep this country in birds, showy asters, and the *sing kahkwa*
kalakala
that sagebrush sparrows call song. Below the windy hills,

where snow catches the plum-coloured light at Canim Bay,
the people of the tent camp are ritually preparing the *tmx*^{w}*ulaʔx*^{w} for fire

and practise bathing in it, rubbing it over their naked thighs,
over chests and knotted spines, laying the skin of their necks

out on sand raked clean by harrows to cover the press
of their heels. The work is done well. There are none.

Above their sandy redds, on a ridgeline between vineyards,
a wild dog has pierced a deer's femur with a canine

and dropped it for anyone combing by to stumble on: a message.
I lift it from the ridgeline of glacier-washed gravel

where it has been lowered to the grass,
returned to the kick of hoof above wild plums and red willow,

smell the rank wind in it and then put
it to my two pursed lips and blow to hear its song.

MISERERE

Have mercy upon me, O God. —Psalm 51

Have mercy upon the men of the porcupine grass, my sea, according
to your rain:
according to the multitude of your tender salmon, blot out their
transgressions.

Wash them thoroughly from their fencelines, and cleanse them from
the furrows of their ploughs.
For they walk into the mountains' wing, with their salt fields of
cheatgrass ever before them.

Against you, you only, have they sinned, and hatched this evil in your
sight: that you might
be justified when you speak, and be clear when you rise, and when you
stream as rain.

As you know and see, your people were shaped in a war between
industry and domesticity,
and among the builders of water schemes and industrial apple
plantations, their mothers conceived them.

Behold, you desire the bright bird tail of current in the lost falls of
your rivers:
and in their deeps and blown soils and choked bars, you shall bring
children to know wisdom.

Purge your brood with big sage, with antelope brush and bitterroot, and
your children shall be clean:
wash them with *camash* flowers, and they shall be bluer than mountains
of snow over which caribou pace with their heads bowed.

Wake the hatchlings in your grass to hear the dancing drum of the
desert rain,
that the bones which have been cast back into your waters may rejoice.

Hide your face from their waste orchards and eroded mint fields and
asparagus blocks
abandoned to salt, and blot out all their deeds of ownership.

Create in these children's children a clean house, my sea, and renew a right
spirit within them as they flow down your rivers with your first
silver people.

Cast them not away from your currents, and take not your draining
snowfields from them.
You are still warming from the chill that ground down your shores into
dune grass.

Restore unto your babies the joy of your first floods, and uphold them
with your green channels
through willow and black cottonwood and mosquito thatch and evening.

Then will they teach all transgressors your salt ways, and the enthralled
and the builders
of turbines and the uranium tube processors shall be converted unto you.

Deliver your little tykes from clear-cuts and poison, my sea's rivers, you
channels of the cleansing rains,
and their tongues shall sing aloud of your shores, and flow down to the
moon with women

and their men to be written by the first sandpipers, in the first song that
is ongoing.
O, my sea's rivers of spearmint and horsetails, open your people's lips,
and their mouths shall sing in your praise.

For you desire nothing of their ends; else would they give them: you
delight not in symbolic
offerings nor the video presentations at the glass-scarred Columbia
River museum.

The offerings you have proffered on a wafer of cedar are your splayed
spine:
a broken and a contrite heart, your currents; you will not despise the
hungry.

Do good in your good pleasure unto this house: build you the
walls of this soil and these souls.
Then shall you be pleased with the heart given freely and
completely, haunted

with the ties that bind to an old way of speaking burnt away and burnt
completely;
then shall all people of clear heart step out with you in the moon
of the silver rain,

and meet you at your mouth and theirs, and fly with cormorants,
pelicans, and crying gulls,
rising above men who quote Tennyson as they leave the continent and
become thee, *kátsuk*.

SAYING THE NAMES SHANTY

for Al Purdy

It was Al who said it, to stick out the thumb's knuckle and nail, crook'd,
to say with a gesture where you want to get along to

and see who is going there, too, with her hands on the wheel's leather
and the rubber taking the curves of the Crowsnest,

crossing the line from black tar's unwinding ribbon
into the riddle of headlights weaving between Similkameen deer
    and Arcturus.

That's where we're all going, isn't it, in the passenger seat's
    squeak and creak,
after being picked up in the rain at Snass Creek.

It's you and me in this old Chevy, crossing the Cascades,
going where the heart beats, which is the one trick it knows well,

heading, as Al put it, to Head-Smashed-In Buffalo Jump and
    Whachamacallit,
where I picked chokecherries in the Blackfoot wind

and was emptied and filled in the same moment
the road is eddying across a thousand miles, thinking.

The Tulameen, Al said in his jack shirt,
knocking the road's cap off, the Spillimacheen, the Similkameen,
    tipping it back.

It was Al who gave the words for my tomato field in Keremeos,
beating it out with finger taps on oilcloth in a green-painted kitchen:

his soul, that is, way out there, driving a Malibu over Anarchist to
    Greenwood,
through the black slag heaps to Grand Forks and east,

pushing a fire before him, as he put it, with his foot to the mat,
and Stan Rogers riding shotgun, and then, mercy,

coming on Franklin on the gravel shoulder at Moose Jaw with his
    thumb out.
That's what I'm talking about now, to you who're crossing the
    mountains with me,

who're maybe willing to take the wheel when I nod off on that long
    stretch between Creston
and Field where the pines say the name of the night over and over

and it sounds like the wind talking with two spirits. It is.
The road is its own map, not the other way round, and the names it
    knows us by

are the ways things keep right on going to right on going: q'awsitk^{w} and
    sacred kɫlilx'^{w},
with the thousand eyes, each a mouth for the sky, and the salt between
    them the star road.

Al is still walking with his thumb out there,
his soles crunching as he runs for our chrome handle. The radio

is still catching signals on the bends above sẇiẇs and losing them
    at Midway.
There's no figuring the human heart because it has no limbs and
    no limits.

The mountains are echoing Illecillewaet and ċuṗáq̇, the crackle
of gravel from the wheels bringing us home to the grass *tanse.*

There is no map to the powwow that awaits us at snkx̌ykntn.
We follow the rain
and the light on the mountains, long after the beginning has ended,

and long before even its ends have unravelled to water
and the click click click clatter of trout's knock under the stars' milt
and the flick

of the moon in high current and the cool brush of our hike into the
túkʷtúlaʔxʷ,
to the ones who are waiting to ride us, not to Belleville this time,
not to Al's Canada,

but to sqáx̌aʔ and t'wcin that are the sound of the land saying
the names that bring us home. Our bones, I mean. Our singing.

SONG FOR THE LOVERS

It would be great to be sitting again in that picker's
shack among the peach trees in Cawston,

to arrive in the night, to turn off in the canary grass,
then along the rutted gravel, then fording the creek

with a clattering fender, then killing the engine,
then the lights, in that order, under Aldebaran,

as if you were visiting Solzhenitsyn in exile,
as if there were someone at the end of the road, at Hrafnseyri,
    for example,

who had words for things and could put the world in order
because he had order within him and knew the old dance songs.

I was that man stepping out the door into the darkness
to greet travellers who had crossed the mountains from the city.

To me, the dark wasn't sudden. I lived there,
but to them it was the lifting of the top of the head

and finding not the mind and its avenues
but the stars rising to great heights on the black wings of birds.

To have a mind you could walk into and pick a peach by feel
among black leaves like feathers,

ah, that was not something to be given up lightly,
but I left it young for the machine gun of free verse

that mowed down Gaudier, when the world died
and the universities were rebuilt in concrete.

Now it is late. I find myself telling young poets to run.
There are wild bees in the hills, who live under the earth,

I tell them. They hum and they buzz; they dart and they tremble.
They need no maps because they wear them on their skins:

the electric touch of the sun waving in fronds of grass, in dawn's swells.
The kids are yawning. They want to be tweeting to each other,

I know that, about celebrating body's maps of skin
folding and unfolding, creasing and smoothing out and glistening,

not listening to old farts talking to angels that are simply not there,
granted, although the mind is.

A fancy, eh. Old men know it isn't. They know it contains mind's
        quick grass
braided by deft fingers around a black fire, dried like lamb shank,

and knotted to mind's hook to lure fish from the deep
where heart surges in thought's tides and the moon

lies on the black bottom, blind as her skin.
Who should we tell of the fishing, and who on earth would listen?

Not the young; their verities are there to protect them
from us, granted. And not old men like us, drinking the heart's whiskey.

And not, surely, old women; they know us.
There is only the world. Rilke's lovers might be fighting to leave it,

but someone has to be there with a bowl of plums in the starlight
to receive them, to open the door they didn't know they were building

to the bed in the mountain orchard, for them to nest in, and make
    love there,
that's all in the making, rarely in the finding or searching, and never
    in the thinking,

while the moon casts the shadows of bats across their limbs all akimbo,
on which are written the true maps of the world.

MACADAM SHANTY

Waves, fronds, wings, birds imitating waves and cedar fronds with
    their tom
foolery went on for a long time of long times and are still ongoing.

At San Josef, a serpent still spits poison into the rock's spittoon.
At the breaking of beak at landfall, at Delkatla, Yan, Saouchten,
    and Masset 1,

cormorants rise from shadow. At Meagwan on Dixon Entrance,
with blue enamel kettles and men wading into crab surf, it goes on still.

At Taaw Tldáaw, at the knot, where Raven crafted people from
    rocked shells,
where the shore is drawn shushed out to the salt of Kaigani Strait,

Klakas, Kassa, Keete, and Nutkwa, all bird talk and toe clack,
all beak clot and eye gravel, where Raven's talkies are tow line

yarding up hammering chain, where he kraks as anchor and forklift,
kraws with ball-peen and tug horn, as each wave talks out its kraaaaaa,

at Yagan and Hiellen Indian Reserve No. 2, it goes on.
Salmon leap rocks, broach rapids, and slip past the Sanpoil,

the Nimíipuu and the Sinkiuse, the Sx̌ʷýʔłpx and the Liksiyu.
June salmon leap through the Nlaka'pamux, the Secwépemc,

the Stó:lō, the Tŝilqot'in, and the Ktunaxa with their nets
of hand-tied cedar root and cinquefoil. Surf spills through the
    black bears

of Nikoamen, caught, split open, dried in the sun, and hung
from rafters, for winter feasts. I lick off my fingers. This whole big house

of fine-beamed cedar, this bentwood box of smolts leaping
out of amber pools between San Francisco and Kodiak,

reeking of sockeye split along the spine of the mountain range's angelus
and the river that carries it to Shaltuuch and Chekwelp, goes on.

Chinook, sockeye, chum, pink, coho, and the steelhead
swim past the hand-tied flies and hollow lines of fishermen

at Shawniken, Schikaelton, and Kumcheen 1, below the black locusts,
with their rattling bean pods and three-inch spines,

where California bighorns cross the Trans-Canada
to drink rock's rattle by dipping black lips among platinum stone clack

as water reflects the deer hide hills above Bighorn. It goes on
at Skoonkoon, Sleetsis, Klahkowit, and Drynoch, in the Fraser drainage

of the one shore of our one sea. It is from this country
that Looking Glass was driven by men who were useless with horses.

The steelhead pause here, under the pine shadows of Kloklowuck
    and Naykikoulth,
and breathe slowly, resting, the fine flower and feather fronds of
    their gills

sweeping in and out, as crows flip flap overhead, each wingbeat paced
perfectly to each black breath. A coyote lopes across the macadam

roadway to Clapperton, under a barbed wire fence at Agate,
and across the clipped brown winter fields of alfalfa at Dot,

his fur hanging in lumps off his spine, without looking back. Suddenly
he sits
in the timothy field at Nooaitch, to tell the story he came for,
by breathing it,

as liquid steelhead swim up their breath from the cool and dreaming sea,
sons and daughters of the moon. This is our telling

of the one tide that stretches from the surf five hundred miles to the
mountains.
It is no longer a sky of graphite or a chunk of this black sage shore

dropping onto Japan. The sun falls no longer in a fierce rain.
At Yasulúusa and Ímatalam, no longer dressed down in Russian thistles,

no longer rough with erratics, where the Earth roots,
it is no longer. Vast ponderosas no longer

sway in sunlight, rich with orioles,
their branches heavy with cones. Thunder Rising and Springtime

no longer lie together under the branches, beading with sweat;
all their cayuses have been turned into dog food. It is no longer.

SHANTY FOR THE CEREMONY OF TEARS

The storm is upon us. Thunder crushes through our grieving house.
Klatsassin is standing on a cliff at Tŝilhqox Biny, accepting fate,

strewn to the hills, with a *King George* rope around his neck like Orion;
as wolves come down from the high stone of the Chezacut and drink

of the earth where he falls—philosophers of the hair shirt:
such a lot of work, this tearing apart, this pretense; their lips stained red;

Roosevelt not even looking up from his turbines and his knitting.
And then silence. Out of the dark, the first forms of the world,

pure shape suspended in the air. Stars nick up slowly through the night.
In the deeps, a herd of appaloosas thunders above this house,

their feet pounding the grasslands, passing through lovers and around
the Earth
as it turns to the sound of birds flashing out of dawn trees in the hurt
of Grand Coulee;

Thunder Rising and Springtime riding through the molten streets of
Nagasaki
on their way to reservation and death, Fat Man going up around them
as they trudge,

heads down, unable to hold out any longer at Havre; remembering,
in their last flicker of consciousness, the particulate light of the one river

pouring down to the one sea and dawn the colour of black sage and
bunchgrass;
their cries heard only by the engineers of the 300 Area, then pushed
into the bleak

black heart of B Reactor, with the returning rains of the river
diverted over them at 250 pounds per square inch of pressure;

where there were once salmon, where there were once black fish
moving through starlight,
to cool their anger beneath the peach trees in Kettle Falls,
Oregon Territory,

June 14, 1940, Chief Jim James attending, in the Ceremony of Tears.
They are with the last salmon and steelhead six years later,

banging their heads against the feet of Grand Coulee Dam
in the long dying, their minds still in shadows, drunk on the cool
morning air,

struggling to fulfill their Treaty Rights, to live as men and women on
this earth
that has been remade into the sun. Wrapped in their trade blankets
woven with whale oil,

they are going on hoofing it on the great exodus of rain back to the
shingle,
where every singer is blinded and blindness roars with the
polyphloesboean

sea caressing the land's cheek, its hem and its small ankles,
miraculously still singing with the blue whales and dark

starlight above the water, waiting for the sun to rise above the desert,
for the return of radioactive salmon, crab-trapped grey whales,

and stuttering blind green sturgeon. The sun is closing over Pášx̣a,
Tamalám, and Dixie, playing its last licks on the bone slide,

right through the legs of the ghost soldiers in blue at Big Hole,
right through the black mouths of their rifles.

WILD DOG SHANTY

In a day that begins with the chit of a siskin and the chirr of blackbirds,
I whistle up the men who kept their own council,

who rode two days through dry washes where ranchers shot each other
over hayfields to listen to the weather in the far mountains,

in the *kwan kwan illahie,* the far land of the thunder.
They came to hear when to cut hay and when to go grouse hunting,

when the snow would fall sideways, how long it would stay,
and how long its going would take.

A man talking on paper, though, ah,
now, that's a snow bunting in a grain field, isn't it,

first here, then here, and here, and then over
there, then there instead, while the coyotes are still

teaching their pups how to howl in the evening,
still kicking them out for a day and letting them discover

the world for themselves, on its own terms. There are things
that the wild dogs of the hills just solve by howling.

Isn't it that our old selves are also chatting and chittering: a western
bluebird bursting out of a hole in an aspen sprout and vanishing
in the sky?

With white clouds and ants going up and down there on the sun's hair?
Right now, the geese are slipping off their bodies

and stripping off their bones, winding their nerves into skeins
and forming words deep in their throats,

honk, honk, honk, honk, honk, honk, honk, honk.
I am walking beneath them forever.

LOOK AT YOU SHANTIE

Today, grasshoppers are click-clacking in their bone song
and lung chant, and the crickets are moaning.

I was given a name by people who came from across the sea.
For sixty-five years, I have been unbuttoning this self,

slipping it off my shoulders, hanging it on a hook
behind a door, unhooking my skin, tugging its tucks and folds,

its wefts and fringes, its eyelets and eyes, its wafted
darts and scars over my head, and letting it catch the shh shh of the wind.

Now I am walking the Earth at the same pace it is walking me.
The only ones talking now are cottonwood leaves above the horsetails:

the world the dead are naming by blowing air through my teeth,
skit skit skit skit skit, as the vesper sparrow puts it, putting it.

A green sweat bee dances around the stamens of a mariposa lily,
gathering up the sun to fly it into the soil to feed her wiggling larvae.

A rockfall's crack, clatter, and dust tell what they know from the
    moment I know it,
that the sky is a shaman looking out at me, that I look back, trilling.

When I was young, I lay under a ponderosa's net of roped feathers.
Its mare's tail brushed my face as it caught the sky out of season and
    needled,

while the back of my head opened into the Earth's shhhhhhhhhhhh!
I wafted for a moment through grey light, forever; through sheets

of rain that fall across the clear air of the valley in April, in music,
and every moment they had lived was open to me to follow. I followed.

Then I opened my eyes to the sun.
In all ways, she was ponderosa: hawk, standing.

It was no dream. A pine reaches for the light
without seeing it: a river flowing in air. Hair.

The world is a white egg, speckled with dust.
It takes a lifetime to become the Earth. There is a long process

of becoming a self and then a longer process of setting it aside
so that the emptiness it made and filled can be filled with the sky.

The dead shuttle back and forth, up the aspens and back down in the air,
dragging the sea out of skin, carrying it home over the mountains.

Magpies are flap-flapping from treetop to treetop, casting a net
of nerves over the country that is made out of the quarter tones

of bone's knock-knock knock-KNOCK, the storied step
from toe to heel and heel to kick kick kick kick kick kick

in grass's pricked mirror going on going on going on.
That is the way of talking here

between the whorls of the memory thought walks through:
claws tick-ticking on stone; blue

feathers black in the light, the whole sky
whirling by staying still still. A river

of milkweed down arcs between today's wind and tomorrow's.
Featherlesss robins open their mouths again and again in the chill.

In night's green field above the house I made in the fire pines' soot black,
the dead are speaking with the mouths of their hands on hearts of
    bone and skin.

Look at you walking there with them across the ice, on the star road,
with a bird in your throat, and on the road of the waters, with a char.

Look at you, all barefoot, all silver.
Just look at you. Look at you now.

ROUND FOR THE MIND OF THE WORLD

The sky clears and things that seemed so solid blow off in scudding clouds:
the sandhill cranes of the Mackenzie Delta catch the plateau wind's measure.

A loon floats on the morning after the lake turns over, so blue,
then dives in to practise flying, first under the water, then above it.

There is no country on Earth that lasts longer.
The loon answers with the whole breadth of lake and sky:

the rain's pit pats plashing on the lake's
uplifted face, its breath mask.

When a drum is speaking, only the drum is speaking.
There is a tradition of answering it so it doesn't fall too quickly.

Trout leap into air and fall back gloved with the sun.
All identity is erased when you are naked in starlight.

The fear of losing your self and becoming an anthill passes.
Soon you are bound to the earth, to spring melt in the coulees,

the síyaʔ blossoms of April, May's grubs, and June's fruit,
weaving our fingers out of willows bright with goldfinches.

All of us star creatures are one breath climbing the ladder of horsetails,
all one boy crushing it between finger and thumb

and making a whistle: that cry the lips know
of a grouse, as breath explodes out of them with an oh.

Brothers, sisters, come to the dance now, and again.
Our hearts are beating here together; we are flying

wingtip to wingtip, buffleheads gathering on the marshes in Autumn,
all of us together the grass taking wing above Vaseux and sqáx̌aʔ,

some of us spirit and some of us dwelling in bodies, but all of us living,
all of us the husk of the filbert, the nut in its shell,

and the crow knock knock knock knock
knocking at the rattling wooden mind of the world.

TRUTH AND RECONCILIATION SHANTY

There is the way a man who walks barefoot is mad to those who
    wear boots
and those who smoke tobacco aren't working hard enough to the
    hard drinkers,

but there is also the manner in which a man rises with the sun,
walks through the sun all day, and holds it all night.

Say what you like. It makes no difference if there is weight to the world,
or if dust is weightless. The bones are hollow, that a man flies with,

and as for feathers, boots won't help them grow, and as for horses,
    they run.
Some men leave them wild on the =sqáx̌aʔ benches, and others tin them.

That's the way of it: no one owns them. As for the Spaniards,
you must have heard of the mound of helmets with its mouth shut,

where the Keremeyeus River enters the main valley. No matter.
No one knows the where of that, except those who are not saying,

nor should you, whatever you call yourself: man, woman, soul,
    heart, think,
womb, cock of the walk, citizen, whatever, wherever, whenever you
    wheeze and sweat.

There is the way a woman cracks dogbane, that comes from long practice,
the way she rolls it on her thighs, as the land does, into cord, half salt:
    rivers.

The sea receives them, but that is not their point. They have none.
They are peachleaf willow and bullheads and pebbles.

The brown reed that grows at the marsh edge once brought in steelhead,
sturgeon, salmon, and pink-bellied kokanee, teeming,

and made the lassoes that Lucy Simla's boys used to yard in cattle.
All other records are kept by the dead, who are not talking, are they,

even though your listening is their listening and your speaking
    their speaking,
here where we are halfway between coming and going

in our coming and going. Some questions aren't questions.
Some answers aren't gifted in answer.

There is the way that is the way of it and the way that is no way at all:
the border that keeps me awake nights with its sodium lights and
    drug dogs.

When I went in for my industrial schooling in the new shirt sewn by
    my mother,
Kojoti's pups kicked the shit out of me in the hopscotch corner kids
    pissed in.

One went on to fame on the hip hop circuit. Another got all tangled
up in the barbed wire on an after-school grouse hunt, bang,

and all the time we had our fingernails and ears checked every
    morning for dirt,
were rapped across the knuckles with a steel-edged ruler by Mrs. Farmer,

and received the instruction that passed for wisdom: civilization
was better than living on Earth as one of its creatures

because instead of moving house with the seasons, you got a corn
broom and swept.
There were illustrations. We learned to read by learning to read that,

but not how to read which flat rock up ahead a rattler would find you on,
as you climbed the twelve-thousand-year-old trail up the cleft in Kobau
Mountain.

That we had to learn on our own. About the two-headed rattler,
the one that moved between worlds, a kind of portable peyote, well,

no one told us about that, or of the nights when there was no moon,
then we got to see the salt sifting in the currents of the river,

when we were fish hugging its bottom stones and all the wind was water.
For the love of wheatgrass, that is what is meant by reconciliation,

that is how to stand on the six hundred generations washed over by
the flood river,
that is the body the Earth blows through as wind,

male, female, neither, both, even changing from morning to evening,
sweating out smoke and grease when the Bear settles in its knuckles
to stay,

that is how to breathe starlight and how to see by it,
which is no small reckoning, which is no little honour.

We are all just trying to survive here, whether playing war under the
cottonwoods,
with agreement between cowboys and Indians that the enemy
was that Kraut,

caught between enemy lines, which meant beatings, pummellings,
    dog piles,
kicks to the groin, and all the pain of the residential school system,

that carried, at least, an honest and ritual message.
Every dog knows, on every hilltop, this yap yap.

It had to be like that. That was our breaking. And look at us now,
more than half of us already turned to a thread of sage smoke,

rising up into the sky's hole. Take a whiff: pungent.
That's who we are, not who we were. Who we were is children.

HUNGER SHANTY

In '29, Bruno Leipe fled the Nazis and gave me a chance at being a
whippersnapper,
with third-class steerage on a refugee ship out of Hamburg.

It's been ninety-four years but he's still in it, practising knock-knock jokes
and falling in love every minute. I have his Confucius in its slip sleeve

and his motorcycling jacket. There's time for poverty later.
Although my people were washed from the coal fields between
Dresden and Auschwitz,

and naked in the sky I am as dark as a gypsy in a vardo clop clopping
from one shtetl to another, banging my tin pots and whistling,
I am no breeder

of genetically modified apples that stay white on the counter.
I was Puck, first, and then Cernunnos, and then I walked away from
plutonium altogether.

Look, this is the yarn: my mother and hers, Bruno's bobbed Titania,
Martha,
who ran a theatre in Breslau and followed her Oberon to the ends
of the Earth

to live in a hand-built house among Norwegian Lutheran dreamers.
She brought the morning's raspberry pick down to Stó:lō women at
Mission.

In the hands' mirror, they gave her *chikamin pish* to take home, woman
to woman,
out of pity, out of their common birthright, and she accepted

their ancestors to feed her daughter, who birthed me in turn out of their skitter
of scales that covered the whole kitchen, and her tears,

to put up in the glass sealers called gem jars, which she
carried down into the darkness and then fought the spiders back

to bring up again in the winter, and that's what they lived on,
that gesture. Was that poverty? No, that was Potlatch.

It was Bruno who put it best: a real communist never fought for rights.
It was work he was after. Communism was a program of economics,

not the disrespect of one woman saying to another
that her choice to raise children within a story of her own making

was not heroic, not a way of stopping
history right there by the force of her will. A fairy tale?

Hardly. When Martha connived with a communist *Genossin* in Penticton
to drag her guitar player and his heart attacks south out of exile,

and finally had a small house with a fireplace of green brick in Naramata,
she still had raspberries, except now I was the young'un chosen to pluck them.

It was I who swatted mosquitoes under the red sun and popped drupes through
the gap between my front teeth. Poverty and all of its moral lessons came later.

In that old British Columbia, there was no poverty. There were Kojoti's
 shit piles
at sx̌ʷəx̌ʷnitkʷ, talking to the stars in the Earth's winds,

that lingo I have spent a lifetime learning: the plunge a loon makes
into the green light below the earth's lid, mating; the cry.

For a while after that, there was Burl Ives on the hi-fi
and bear meat on Martha's table; every second man

you met had been a partisan, and the rest had been soldiers
fighting the Nazis who fill a place in the popular

imagination right beside Baba Yaga, who ate iron
nails for breakfast and then suckled Death at her teats;

soon there was just the way one group of men sold the world of another
and called that progress. It wasn't.

It was just old Väinämöinen, the smith, with two skulls in his codpiece
and a river boat knocked together out of his sprung rib cage.

It was just a monster out of the ancient love poetry laid down in Sanskrit,
that will never be equalled.

It was never that way for my mother
with her yellow braids dipped into ink wells.

It was bread. And freight rates. You didn't buy something like that.
You asked for it from the Earth, and the Earth gave it,

after the wind blew through it and lifted it and dropped it in the
waves of the sea.
It was yeast. It was the work of women in their kitchens. Poverty
came later.

The first rule of a Potlatch: when you come, have your hands open,
and when you come again, come with your hands open.

The goal of a society of things is to make people into things.
The goal of a society of people is to be people.

The goal of living on the Earth is to be the earth.
The goal of heaven is to become it.

A closed hand cannot hold an open heart.
In the flow of a river to swim is to breathe faster.

At some point, a man has to stand up for some particular conception of
what it is to be human.
The first need, the one that matters, is hunger.

The great drum of the sky tells the brushing through stalks
that names it as sound, the bluebunch wheatgrass

that is the scales of a salmon snouting up the stars in their beds,
a way of weaving and knitting and sticking

the map of wildflowers every child leaves in her footsteps
if left to the world, if the world is left to her.

The weaving goes on with one half of your mind read by your hand
and the other by your other hand. I bring them together now, clapping

the lip of the Earth that birthed me by putting
one hand into the hand of another and feeling the spark of the grass there.

It isn't about speaking. The water beetle walks on her hands,
making of the water and the light on the water the cloth

of Black Sage spilling its milky sand into the Pacific's chalk maw
and the surf hurling it back, smelling of clams,

and so the land is born from the water
just as water is born from the sand.

WISDOM SHANTY

There is a people who have named this country after a dissection of light.
They bandy words around like six guns: Nature, they say, and Physics.

They slosh white sauce on biscuits and hammer
poetry out of the pattern of shotgun blasts on road signs:

Sharp Curve Ahead, Slow to 40, No Parking on Shoulder.
Their sons and daughters leave footprints in tilled fields swept by the
    ghosts of horses.

There is the conviction among them that crows don't own Camas Prairie,
that they do. The crows are laughing about that right now.

The punchline? Glyphosate. Caw caw caw.
When the old summer moon snags in the ponderosas, these folks

sing *Oh my darling, Clementine, your ruby lips above the water.*
I sing along. I, too, am from this country. I cut my teeth on glyphosate.

There was a wine called Similkameen Superior.
Back in the day, we named it Roundup. This is the secret

known by all winemakers: bring out one bottle of the good stuff.
After that, everyone will be happy to drink gun cleaner.

Then it got weird: Pinot Meunier, people say, Muscat Ottenel,
    patio sipper.
There is a precise moment at which champagne yeasts,

digesting grape juice, turn to black pepper.
It is a prick on the tongue. Winemakers

catch it and call it terroir: the land rising in bubbles.
Forgive them. They really do think they own their vineyards.

Starlings know better. There is a people who make a flag of a tree
that is a salmon climbing the ladder of rain and describe

the chert quarries of Cau'amuitk as volcanic extrusions—
not as moon's milk, not as pine pitch bubbling out.

Those people love logic but they've never chewed it.
Isaac Newton gives them a shiver in the mosquito thatch of evening,

when the air is woven into the whine of nerves and the grain
barges are going east and west through the locks below them.

Smart people go in. Fools start swatting.
For the abandoned sons of abandoned orchards, myself included,

the Nčí Wána carries the desert of spade-footed toads into the Pacific
and then drops it like hot bannock.

The Cascades, men called the gate of the mountains.
I did, too, on my first trip upriver. Forgive me.

It was my first step into emptiness. Now I live there.
People drive east from Portland on Saturdays to sip pinot on wrought-
iron patios,

which is secret code for raw cotton dresses tasting of mango,
lemongrass, and quince. Hey, maybe

they have never gnawed their way into yeasty bread
pulled from the oven in a snowstorm in December, smeared with
fruit butter,

or followed hawks following them walking to eat what they scare,
but what does that matter: quince is mineral, it's bitter,

and every loaf from the Horse Heaven, north of Roosevelt,
way up there where the sky thwacks the Earth's rump,

is ripened with that old weed killer glyphosate: a mineral salt.
If you speak of terroir, know it.

There is a people who have named this country after California,
which is named after France which is named after France,

and they want their merlot to smack like blackberry jam:
those penny candies we used to buy at Ike's at lunchtime,

son of a blue opium bottle full of threads of grey mildew.
History is not the point, nor is the rain drawn by gravity

through movement to stillness. I get up in the morning like other men;
I lay me down with my body at night and pray for forgetfulness

to come quick and the waking to be the deep water at Wallula,
and the white sturgeon, who carry the stars in their bellies.

It's the absence that gives the rain motion,
the motion that gives absence stillness,

the stillness that is the ponderosa
following the rain in the dark on the ladder of carbon, up to the sun.

Newton split light with prisms, then said, That's light.
No, it was prisms.

I used to say Canada and the USA were countries.
No, they were prisons.

When I find a clutch of eggs under the bunchgrass, I don't look anymore.
It's what Janice Frank taught me in a break from spirit wrestling

with Secwépemctsín in a green classroom: respect is earned because
    it is given.
To the class of priests called anthropologists, this is called gambling,

but in my country, men speak for themselves, and the redfish, and
    the sparrows,
and they listen to their mothers, even when they have gone to spirit,
    even

when they are hail striking grass like pheasants tiptoeing through
    the coyotes,
just so, just so, just so and they're gone,

when everything is their presence, when a man learns his limits
and then carries past them as something more than he was when he
    began walking

and asks nothing but what has already been given: chert on the ridges,
    and hands
that have been grasping it since salmon first offered wisdom.

MARBLE MOUNTAIN SONG

There were the years we looked forward to making the world new.
Every morning I wake to watch you sleeping only skin deep,

and the ocean in you rises and falls, each time for the first time,
    thank God.
There are loons in the lake we left and came back to,

and the light that is the sky touching the earth inside us,
outside us, who cares: touching. Details mean nothing on the lake
    at 6 a.m.

when the fish leap into the air over and over.
Small things, I guess, but there's a time

when a man and a woman are just a man and a woman
and talking is just talking,

when the ancestors are silent for a spell, holding their breath, waiting
to see what the kids will say when they grow into their voices.

I'm waiting for that, too. The lake practises flight. Soon the grebe
that met me on the water this morning will be a different grebe

and I won't be there to greet it or to tell you of the proud lift of its head,
and all that curiosity and sureness, but I am now.

WEIGHTLESS SHANTY

There's no point any longer, not at my age, of carrying
the weight of the whole world on my shoulders. I'm not Atlas.

The world is not a globe, either, with latitude and longitude marked
    with a protractor.
It's appetite. Let me keep za'atar and sumach, the old ones the
    colour of dawn,

with incoming sails running before the wind at sunset, cut by the
    Earth's angle,
break fast with sunrise and shed this damned weight.

It's time for flatbread and oil in a clay dish.
It's time for oregano to bloom and chicory

that lures green bees to the roadsides with its white pollen.
There was a time, in Earth's memory, when there was no Monsanto.

I went to the white shells of alkali on the bottom of field stones
and read the map of the world there. I hoed tomatoes and onions.

In my valley deep under the Cathedrals I did the real work
in a place with names and histories of its own.

I still have that in my heart's pouch and my lungs' branches.
I worked with a rice planter from Saskatchewan

under skies that were bluer than the overturned dish of the kibbutz.
Evenings, we opened up the *Tao* under a sumac as the stars took us.

In those days the sun still settled at Acnulox,
back into the Earth's core: a peach pit.

In the starlit embers that followed re-entry, the trees flew in the dark.
    I flew with them.
Bats wove around me, and within me. They still do.

We were the ones who stayed with the Earth in those years, when that
    was still a culture,
and if a distant society [*sic*] licked its finger and stuck it into a socket,
    what was that to us?

The Mica Dam was on the other end of that thing.
Jesus! What were they thinking?

I didn't have much time to contemplate such madness,
I thought. I picked apricots before the sun. I watched

the sun rise within them, felt them warm with the day under my hands
and burn like coals into the green clouds of the evening

in that one week in the summer when time was not what you made of it
but what it made of you. A man, I mean. A woman. A tree,

god, it's all the same thing, with its branches opening into the
    Sməlqmıx wind.
We had a history with no bottom. There was no end to the world

in any direction, all the way up to c̓up̓áq̓, the mountain,
the frightened girl watching the stars turn in the great wheel we, too,
    were watching.

The magnetic Earth's core lay on the soil's surface,
so hot you couldn't put your foot down. We breathed a blast furnace.

The sky tasted of rock vapour. We were the Sun's people. We were
its horses.
Now people who stepped out of TV screens are running the world,

as they call it, giving workshops on the lack of place in place,
how there is no here in here and there in there. They teach

our children that no place is everywhere, but they are just not saying
beefsteak tomatoes are now grown under plastic

to make them accord with the seasons in Middle England,
and the work of a man's hands is now owned by Monsanto,

or that glyphosate's salty crystals in your gut give you cancer.
They actually think they have the right to speak for Earth's children

in her last days, who knew the sun and moon
and the tomato hornworm that makes the luna moth in the delphiniums,

when we were transcendent and bringing children into the Sun's song.
Even after all these years you can still

smell it on the wind. Then you go down
to the water and watch the bears cross and cross it.

SHOTGUN SHANTY

For ten autumns in the roar of the river tumbling stones
I walked with Homer and Virgil. Poetry was an unbroken tradition

that followed the fall of the feet on earth's dithyrambs and iambics,
its trochees and scree clatter at Paul Creek,

when goats stopped and looked down at me from the cliff faces
then went about their own business. I didn't think it needed to be said.

I thought it was obvious. I went off to raise children in the sky,
on the shore of a lake shining with fire under Earth's lid.

I thought there was respect for this knowledge in Toronto and
        Mississauga.
I thought Canada was a place made out of knowing. Fool, me.

Up there in the sky, though, we were all raising our children together,
and at 5 p.m. all spring and summer the eagle came by, riding a thermal,

and sometimes it thundered and the house shook and we held tightly
        to each other,
at one with the swallows outside our window,

and it is not again to be met with.
Our country began to be ruled by the mayors of Vancouver,

who gave it over to a talk show host, and our daughters learned English,
forgetting word by word their first language,

all loon talk and the high cry that carries across the plateau
in the wake of the thunder. When I came down from the fire country,

down snk̓y̓ép's yack, down through the dreamtime of Basque,
Cook's Ferry, and Spahats,

I was told that *The New Yorker* was a local magazine, and the rest of it,
  the world,
was *nada*, nothing, and everything I took to be poetry was intellectual
  pretension.

It was meant as a consolation. I had met the global diaspora,
not in a slow awakening but in all of five minutes;

not as a liberation but as the end of the Earth.
That was the year the Yankees won the war for the Northwest,

after two centuries. I should have seen it. I'm sure sorry I didn't,
but at least I had those years when I still lived with my ancestors,

when we were all hammering bog iron, forging the star road,
boating our skeletons down the soul's platinum rivers,

when the heart was a coal we fanned in a wooden bucket
to keep it burning. I took my models from poets

driven to madness by the Pacific's combers,
who kept the flame alive in the temples of the skull by blowing on it,

and saw the ocean as a story, not a management area.
Now Homer Simpson runs the poetic committees and Big Bird

the departments of philosophy, not the sandhill cranes
stitching the world together in the oldest of stories

and catching their breath. Now I have the last
apricot tree between here and Smolensk. I serve her.

Let me stay with the Earth until she has done weeping.
Let me love her green bees and her magenta lilies,

while my whole generation and all those that followed,
teeming in their multitudes, are shuffling paper responsibilities,

raking leaves while the town's true poet, John,
a man as sane as a fence post, barbed wire, and a staple,

is locked up with the drug kings in the halfway house behind the sewage
lagoon and the bottle depot, because nobody else will have him,

seeing as he is honest and says what needs to be said
about beauty and honour and memory, and the loss of it.

He was once the gardener to a painter. She is much celebrated
as a prisoner in a house on the hill. Few talkers ever

garden her paintings. John chucks his poems into boxes.
I have them here, for safekeeping, after he burned his last bridges.

Way up in the bush outside McLeese there's another poet, another
    friend of horses,
with hair as wild as a cottonwood in a windstorm.

He puts his poems into boxes, too,
pounded out on an old Corona as if he were a spy behind the Iron
    Curtain, in Brno,

and nobody sees them, although he is the one
true seer between Fountain and Moscow,

a horse logger who knows his way around a Percheron and the
    pool table
he keeps above its barn, in between snorts of whiskey

left by those who come to pay their respects.
If you hear a strange click click on cold nights

when the thermometer plummets to forty,
you know that's Lorne playing snooker with Kojoti, and winning.

He lives under the waste rock of Gibraltar Mine that scrapes
copper out of the plateau, so people can build houses

in Florida, so others can go bankrupt in the beautiful
music that is international finance and instant communication,

which could be called poetry, too, couldn't it,
of course it could, except that it isn't.

There were poets before us. They weren't Canadians. They sang about
    this place,
and anything else is just a prairie dog blowing bagpipes made of old
    Eaton's corsets.

Now poets own universities. Look, I'm not sure which way it goes in
    the tangle
of limbs and buttocks and tender celebrations of creativity and
    individual realization,

but they sure as hell don't study the ravens' *kalook* and their click clack.
They are something they could find in a book, and... I think that's about it.

Maybe they have, I mean found themselves there, in the white space
    between the lines.
Stranger things are possible, like mantis flies, that live off spiders' blood,

and mosquitoes that eeeeyew. And love? Well,
who's going to listen to an old guy losing his hair,

who learned poetry from a peach tree, was typecast as Puck,
taken up by fairies, and then went on a walkabout,

which has lasted some forty-six years now, which,
to strip it naked and wipe its arse, sprinkle on some talcum, swaddle it,
    and sing

Sleep baby sleep, is exactly the span during which a new world has
    been born,
like Jesus. And me? I'm walking with the shamans tonight,

trit-trotting behind them with this one message in clear:
we are what we love and where we have loved it.

There was never anything in books that wasn't better off
when you opened its latch and shooed it. Poetry

was just a reason to keep talking and to keep drinking the Moon's
    whiskey.
It could make a human out of you, or kill you,

which is pretty much about the same damn thing in the end.
This isn't some slave republic

turned into an oil sump and yammering for pipelines,
but a knocking on the door of the heart, and the stepping in

when it opens, into the bathhouse.
For the love of all things decent, don't cover up.

The steam is rising and your lovers are waiting with a gourd for the water
to pour itself over your beautiful skin and for you to direct it

to her, or him, or them, to trickle and glisten
as it streams down over back, breast, buttocks, thighs, and ankles

into the wooden floor and through it into the veins of the earth,
that no one needs to melt down and extrude into three wire copper

to carry a current between a river and a smart phone.
If you're staying, stay. Learn Secwepemctsín,

one word at a time, like I did,
and then forget it all at once, as I did, too,

and then struggle to bring it back with the only thing you have:
your one word heaped onto another, with a chunk of corn on the side

and a lump of bannock and a flank of salmon,
under the basketball hoops at Tsq'éscen', with the elders.

BELLA CIAO SHANTY

In the green light of the world, the swallows weave the world above and the world below,
as Ezra put it from Rapallo when he was halfway down Dante's stair

into the dark ventricle where men pace, swinging their heads as lanterns.
He was fifty-eight. I'm older.

When men came to his door without knocking,
with their collection of antique bird rifles and a Marxism

they had learned in the mountains,
he stuffed his Confucius into his pocket and followed.

He had already retreated from the church bells of Kensington.
He knew the millefiori and the cross-stitch the women of the fin de siècle

worked in front of coal scuttles and fire screens
of hand-hammered copper. He knew that authenticity

was to make yourself into a ceremony of ashes.
History doesn't just contain Caesar,

accepting murder over a return to the Senate.
It also houses Tiberius,

hurling his blonde German slave girls off the cliffs
of his palace for kicks, and the way the circlet

of traffic at the heart of London before the wars
spreads out to the twin hearts of the world,

to sx̌ʷəx̌ʷnitkʷ and Tk'emlúps, remaking them into its own image. Look,
now, the geese are flying in the morning light

and the blackbirds are chirring in the mountains,
each the only blackbird in a world that is opening everywhere at once.

Ezra is known now for the shotgun scatter he made of words,
the shell fragments they represented of moments of unified being

lobbed one after the other at the bastions of civilized syntax as people
trudged out of the darkness into its mouth and oblivion: Paris.

It was the same for me when I sat down with a lizard
at Rilke's grave at Raron and talked about things of the greatest significance:

the wind in the grass along the path up from the stacked stone houses
    of the village,
drawing the air of half of Europe up to the vineyards above Visperterminen

and from there into the blue air above Italy;
how wine cupped in Roman glass pours out of the Earth's breath

and Nature is an old thing, abandoned, and broken:
a garden but not of human fashioning, overgrown,

with its spirit caged in a tree trunk,
smashed open, released like perfume.

We have all been taken away from our language until we forgot
that we even spoke it: and then what?

Then we look to each other.
In the morning, we are going to the mountains.

BEACON ROCK SHANTY

A man is reading his mind in rock that rose before tall firs first
stuck out feathers and sank their hands into Earth's veins.

Mountains dive under the water, before rising to shake out their hair.
In a wool tangle of freeways and a jumble of mountains blown

up by dynamite, a woman holds one end of a Coleman cooler.
Her husband holds the other. They carry their past and future.

In the cooler is ice from the Texaco up the explorers' road, and ancestors
who gave themselves up by following the line to the hand

before they hit the concrete wall, all silver. Far to the east, a woman
guards a border at a Quick Stop with a green dragon tattooed to
    her cancer.

At the heart of the mountains, a woman guards the border between self
and not self with spearmint tea picked from the bed of the glaciers.

In the city of grain terminals they do it with designer dresses and
    Voodoo donuts,
fluffed with sugar and cream, all sweet sixteen.

It is not language that is on the journey, wearing the face of the sun,
sitting on the Beacon Rock State Park boat launch dock dressed in pink

string and laughing, with the men, yet soon cold, alone,
dressing in yellow on evening's asphalt, as naked

as if she were wearing nothing else but her need: this young
    woman's body,
this one who wants to be here and doesn't. It is not our *selves*

who are on this journey. To young souls, the world is a graveyard.
They don't wander between tombstones. They are under Earth's lid.
They want out.

Fair enough, but to old ones, there are rivers, trees, and valleys within the hands.
There are hiking paths in the beds of old railroads

going up to the Brides of the Sun at 105 degrees Fahrenheit,
where the Eel Trail between the rock falls once carried the US Army,

or, rather, the horde that once passed for such an outfit,
when it was led, if one could still hammer the words that way on an anvil,

by the man who invented land mines to keep men in chains to mint juleps,
mountain stills, and old ballads about knights being pecked by ravens.

The dream of all this land becoming a country is a cold storage in Wenatchee,
and a businessman's club that's an art deco arrangement of apartments for seniors,

with pad Thai in the old ballroom and the paint peeling off.
After a while you learn to walk away from all that you held dear,

from any kind of a country—for me, it is the green Top
Red Delicious orchards of Cowiche and Tieton—to sit

with a chocolate lily and a bee. To bumble. To the old,
such things matter. We are on a journey from here to here,

who have no country. To the young,
who still think they have one but no memory,

there are tombstones behind rusted gates,
bound together with wild clematis,

that are none of their doing. The old,
with their hair made of clematis threads,

are fiddling with the rusty latches. They don't
bother about snakes. They don't scare

by the weight meant to put an end to things
that can no longer be put right by living.

The young poets are saying they would never live in Ritzville or Washtucna.
They would never live in 100 Mile House or Squilax.

They are saying the dead live there, or the Confederacy, or Old White Men,
but might they be forgetting their mothers

who picked peaches, until their breasts itched with fuzz,
to bake them into pies in the winter, so they could set

the sun in the centre of their family table and pray to it, just for a moment,
in the name of the Father and the Son and the Holy Ghost,

or just for the sweetness? Might they be forgetting aprons
and gingham and the courage in the face of terror

that made them? Isn't this all a Potlatch?
We bring casseroles, and bread, and blankets,

because we are nothing without each other.
Without each other, we are nothing.

It doesn't matter how you say it: what the dead know
is there is honour not won in battle. They know

there is cloud, in which men read the river
as it flows over the peaks of mountains.

They know that even flat, a mountain is the sky's home,
even when it is a seabed,

even when it is the molten heart of earthquake.
They have no fear, even when they are on the road of the soul

between what can be seen and what cannot but is no less real for it.
They are the ones down at the river,

splashing water on the skies they carry with them on their journey,
        their faces,
to see, for an instant, through the air into air,

even when ants walk across it, bearing their larvae,
moving house and hill from one pile of hot gravel to another,

even when they are the kind of knowing that comes from the Cherokee
Trail of Tears pole bean that women tended like a fire

once they trudged out of the Missouri to plant in the Champs Pays,
to forget the passage. We are all in the dark and the pity.

The hands that strike the skin of the light are not ours but our mothers'
and our fathers' who loved them, even badly.

There is the dance and there is the dancing, and they are the same thing,
even when we get the steps wrong and the watchers burst out laughing.

Whatever philosophy we pull over our heads and stick our arms through,
we are still naked, still going down to the river, still climbing the rock,

all of us together, the living and the dead
and those walking between them, shaking

the dry seeds in our bone cups, waiting for thunder,
calling, calling, calling, calling, calling, calling, calling, calling,
then lightening.

CHILCOTIN SINGALONG

a reconciliation dance

I am brushing through the grass of my teeth's rockfalls,
singing rain with my hair tossed back. I am sparking rain with my mouth,

and the tongue in my mouth, and the lips that are the curtains of the heart.
I know long ago the question was asked by people who walked
down the river

into unknown country, so far they became their journey.
The question has been lost, but I have come with this answer,

which is its asking again. Will we, who are walking through the sun
as it weaves the needle-and-thread grass and the blue-green algae

that made the sky, take the *King George* to court when the last
oolichan swims up the tidewash past the spit of salt water?

And when we all do, will we each find a suit at the Sally Ann, one
that's still in style,
with lapels neither too *pitchah* nor too wide, that we can wear to
the trial?

Should we stop breathing the wind to wear a Stampede stetson or an
International
Harvester ball cap with a crumpled brim to the swearing-in

or just slick our hair back so we don't create distrust in the eyes
of the gentlemen *pe* ladies of the jury? Will there actually *be* a jury?

Of our peers? Who have no self, not grass and sky? Really?
Okay, then what promises will we be able to make with our hands and
our fins,

and which of them will we promise to keep, and which
will we actually stand behind, when the cameras are turned off,

or are we that sow who lined up her red cub and her black cub on the
haul road
to get a look at the man who stood there so they could get a good look
at him?

Have we become so enamoured of the glitter of the abandoned
log trucks along the cliffs above the Williams Lake coulee that we have
become strangers

to the niceties of speaking in public? Would it be more appropriate
to speak Punjabi with the men on the green chain on the
Soda Creek Road?

Should we admit that love is tearing us to the four corners of the Earth?
Or should we appropriate buckskin fringes and hang dream catchers

from our mirrors, as we've been told to do,
so bored kids don't torch our RAV4s in the scrub pines south of Puntzi?

And in what subdivision, exactly, should we park our house trailers with
the sagging porches,
and who, precisely, from the Ministry of Children and Families

or the Ministry of Forests or the Ministry of Natural Resources or whoever
minds our sorts of familial goings-on is going to mind

our kids while we get out the duck tape and try to patch the earth
back together again under the hot spot throwing up its cinders at Nazko?

Why is there no Ministry of Wilderness seeking to turn itself into
    the mirage
between sea urchin and cactus, the wind that sighs the warp and weft

of our coming to sand? Who on Earth started the rumour that some of
    us don't live here?
Should those of us who have one play the Métis card right about now?

What about the Land Is Our Mother card? Isn't that all of us?
Would today be the right time to put all of our *chikamin* on *la tahb*—
    the table—

with our hammered-on antlers, our truck *klehs*, our brass
belt buckles with the horse heads, and the lint from our pockets? No?
    What about later?

Or would it be appropriate to call as a witness just one of the 110 sockeye
allotted this year at Farwell, where kids burned down the bridge with
    that bonfire,

as a gift to ease our way through the intricate maze of land claims litigation?
Should we tell the *King George* the real story of that conflagration? I mean,

supposing we knew it? Would a grass *tanse* be in order at Gustafson,
or just a fancy dance, with the mirrors sewn into the beaded breastplates,

here, and here, and here again,
and the one-two-one-two-three footwork, toe to heel and then toe to

heel to toe to heel to toe or was it something like that, was it?
Do you like the cool heart of the ponderosas, that tastes like thunder

cresting a ridge in the Salmon, where the surf turns back into wind?
Do you like the fry bread at Don't Panic We Have Bannock

better or worse than the Cree Aters' at Splatsin?
Do you like the way the *glease* lingers on your lips

long after you've eaten it? Do you lick your fingers?
Should the judges be served first, with the elders, or later, with the kiddies?

Should all the people, mule deer included, along the dust tracks and
    the worn stone
stepping down to the green throat at Xatśūll,

where the sky becomes the flick of a *pish* tail, bring up
the matter of the obsidian trade collapsing four thousand years ago

because it was just too much work and nobody remembered
the strike angles, anyway, and what the hell,

it wasn't worth starting a war over, was it,
and wasn't there too much killing of one people over another,

when the real game was played with *les animaux* of the dreamtime,
who had all our *sticks* lined up in their own hedgerow?

Are we all not weaving our fingers out of grass and grass from our footsteps?
Should we invite the *King George* judge to this *tanse,*

so he can have his feet on our ground, or should we bring him a gift
card for Tim Hortons, or is that bad for his arteries?

How is *that* any different from what has been done to our water
in the industrial hearings surrounding the exploitation

of the Prosperity Claim at Fish Lake, where the trout are as long
as the natural way a *man* sweet-talks a woman but never any longer

and besides does any extra really make any appreciable difference?
Does the size of a village matter?

Should we bring along a bronc rider from Esk'et
to explain just in the way he whooops with his ten-gallon hat

that the idea of a series of pre-land-claim negotiations
with high-priced urban lawyers on both sides of a folding bingo *le tahb*

is preposterous when the *illahie* is a story you tell by walking across it,
and maybe getting a prickly pear cactus stuck in the cuffs of your Levi's

or, worse, in your *derrière*? Because we were speaking French here,
right, or our grandmothers were, long before it became a matter

of political correctness. Who is this we, this *mesika*?
And is there a "them"? Does common law extend to all of us,

even the magpies? Are these appropriate codicils to present to the judge
    in our preamble,
or should we leave them to the main body of our *yiem*, or load them up
    in the appendix?

Don't those things sometimes get inflamed and cut out in Emergency?
Should we be worried about that? Or should we,

the deer people, the dogs and the horses, our bear brothers
and the badgers worrying the hillsides into broken ankles,

just be concerned that the clinic at Alexis is only staffed by nurses,
and there is no paramedic for us between Riske and the Pacific?

And what in the hell does it mean when our grassland benches,
that have supported all of our peoples for two hundred generations,

from the sagebrush wren to the sedum and the lazuli bunting,
are pretty much owned exclusively by one of the principle

sugar daddies of Osama bin Laden? Or is it six hundred generations?
Are we not all brothers and sisters? Are we not all lovers? Do we not

all have hands or wings or leaves or stamens or some damned thing
that can reach out and touch each other? Is there not a string

that we weave between them that is a way of singing?
Spose a man's ancestors came from the plains of Silesia,

or from a *pasiooks* town fiddled away in Eastern Ontar-eye-oh,
where the men used to guzzle gut rot under spreading lilacs in the evening.

Should we not pull him out from Alkali Lake in an October storm
and throw him into a tub and pour scalding water down his spine to
save him?

Are we not memory waking? Are we not the *poh,* the breath,
between earth and the morning *wind*? Are we not wind?

Or should we be setting history outside the boundaries of this parlay,
and how ice *livers* were followed by seas of grass,

then herds of snow-bowed caribou, tracked by hunters,
and goats leaving their fur on the alders, like washing on a Sunday,

and then lone men trading in obsidian, and today the delicate matter
of men playing long-winded poker for rights to tax revenues

a.k.a. mineral resource royalties? Three times? Are they kidding?
Are there boundaries to this discussion? Who sets them? Did you?

As for the bathtub and the nakedness and the exquisite pleasure of
 the hot water,
would you not do the same for us? Is that not why we are having
 this hearing?

To talk about that? Are we not together on this hunt?
Are we not sharing the caress of our hands

on the drum's taught dog face of the Chezacut?
Are we not sharing our beautiful weapons?

SAYING IT BACKWARDS SHANTY

for T.S. Eliot

What if Tom had edited Ezra and his *Cantos* had been set in England
instead of Shanghai
or if he had broadcast over the BBC instead of Radio Mussolini and

hadn't written those funny sad comic books about money, if he
hadn't dealt himself into playing stud poker with bankers? Why,

he might have replaced Bernart de Ventadorn with plough-pulling
John Clare,
and John Adams with Lord Cecil, Marquess of Exeter,

so-called descendant of Elizabeth's Chancellor of the Exchequer,
whose brother settled on a ranch in 100 Mile House, British Columbia,

and in 1947 Anno Domini funded a cult of angelic light and communal
living,
complete with cow punchers and quarter horses and a lime-green
painted kitchen,

and instead of usura and trying to convince the GIs of the United
States Army
to give up on foxholes by reading them the bubble-gum-wrapper poems
of E.E. Cummings,

king of the balloon men, Ez wouldn't have had to speak in tongues or write
with irony. We'd all be playing *s'lahal* now, instead of the sonatas of Vivaldi

that were bombed in Dresden, or dressing in the sweaters
feminists knitted for Marx and Erich Honecker, king of the truly, purely,
industrialized post-humans.

That's water under the bridge. Ezra remains the poet laureate of the
    Paris Métro,
and that boxing match with Hemingway, that took the starch right out
    of him for five minutes,

but not of the Icicle fishery, known now for Wenatchee bratwurst:
    a wasteland.
Imagine, then, if Macavity the Mystery Cat had prowled the
    Chinese cantos

and shredded them into that tinsel dropped from Lancaster bombers
    to jam Jerry radar,
or if Ez hadn't said all those naive things about Europa belonging to
    the Europeans,

and all those hurtful things about the Jews, when he really meant his
    fellow Republicans.
Imagine if Eliot had just emptied that wheelbarrow,

and Ez had been left to write forever about Idaho, and hadn't been driven
by the machine-gunning of sculptors at Neuville-Saint-Vaast

into feeling he had to forever defend poetry against its detractors (bankers),
or if when the chips were down and on one side of the table it was
    civilization

and on the other Čamná, he would have had to choose
salmon drying in the wind night after night. We wouldn't be tippling

Chardonnay with accountants from Tacoma with no polyphloesboean
Aegean of the heart going back to the classics again and starting over
    with nothing,

finding the islands, as Merwin did, with late love and the darkness of
    the body,
that is a light not a shadow. There'd just be dancers on the hill at Waiilatpu

And "'Tis a Gift to Be Simple," with drums holding up fiddles in the
    Champs Pays.
Imagine, just imagine, if Eliot had taken all the kinks out of us, and the
    Greek and the Latin,

and imagine if the lick of our tongues, the *Chinook wawa*,
our first halting knot work, all cohered and the apricot leaves
    stopped falling,

then imagine yourselves standing here, watching them fall at a Wenatchee
without sweet mustard and sausages.

SALISH SEA SHANTY

Children, we who are *salmon* bearing south on our magnetic
  improvisations,
we who are bearing down for Fraser Mouth

and Finn Slough and the chokehold of River Road and Bridgeview,
we who gasp through long bleeding rafts of cedar anchored
  to Snee-Oosh,

where the snow geese speak pure Yukaghir, we,
blind and cold, who are deafened by the heartbreak of the white sea,

who remember still the world before we were our birthing,
with sea suck of gravel, with moan, with wooden hands of water,

the *chuck* is dragging us home from the gene splicers and diviners,
who she shuns, who she sends down among the stones and the
  caddis larvae

for what they have arranged to happen in their name.
She turns in her tracks and drops fish scales behind her:

the path of moonlight across the rippled moon of Frenchman's Pool.
The name of the rain across the tongues of the alders,

the tongues of blue sea urchins and orange sea cats, the purple sea star
and the razor clam that is all tongue,

that is speaking the face of the tide flat,
the *snass* that is the first shook word rising out of Sea's bed,

climbing nightly onto the edge of land at Shelter Bay, then falling,
  exhausted,
rising to the clam gardens of Waiatt and Kanish Bay,

then dropping back, drained, among the feet of the great blue
herons fishing for the rain's people, whooooooOOOOOOOOoooooooo,

she is calling her sisters and their children who gavotte the black channels,
the A pod of Telegraph Cove, the *canim tillicum* of Keecekiltum,

and the children of the rain who swim upstream to their father's
    silver *house,*
the smouldering smelts of the platinum gravel and the men who made

of them the ploughing of the year lived as the sun. She is calling us
calling us calling us calling us calling us, calling, us, home.

PRODIGAL SON SHANTY

for Ezra Pound

Hang it all, Ezra, where were you that day the world ended,
who claimed to be talking to the people?

Why, polishing the chrome headlights of a train in Rapallo, Italy,
and telling everyone that Mussolini had drained the Pontine Marshes.

Well, for what people? Not, surely, for those who threw eagle down on
drowned water.
Ezra, fly home. We need you, you poor blind stuttering Odysseus and
your paraffin candles.

Was your greatest privation of war (your second)
really the need to turn on the Edison, for the first time, in '43?

You poor dumb bastard, stop chattering to the GIs about social credit
and usury,
international Jewry, and the poetry of E.E. Cummings on Radio Rome;

only the FBI is listening and they have no sense of proportion.
Come home, Ezra, and dance with the spinsters of Astoria at the end
of breeding

in their big mahogany-lined house, with its rose bowers gifted to Artemis.
Commit this last indiscretion. Spend your winter season for once

drinking shots of absinthe with its Ladies Flavel on Knob Hill,
where they loved to overwinter away from the rain's wrack and the
bar's drownings.

That old dawg lying on your lintel is It'se-ye-ye, not Virgil.
You were led astray in Europa. *This* is the sea's end.

Let me be Dante to your Whitman and Bernard to the endless
strumming of Dowland to your Anglican hymnal. Shatter us

with your barbarian yawp, you Old Yeller. Walk with us
as the trains scream through The Dalles at midnight, bare steel on
bare steel,

and kids still easing its way with a penny,
picked up again in the morning like a ceremonial Tlingit copper

thrown into the tide's nightmare. It is the Columbia dams that are your
Doge's Palace,
not Machiavelli. Ezra, the headwaters are calling. Put on your red coat

with the moon-hammered silver and the hooked jaw and the hump
and come home to poor drowned Celilo,

where the makeshift spear-fishing decks stare down the concrete wall.
We honour your devotion to the eternal salvation of another ten bars

of the exquisite and virtuoso birdsong of Antonio Vivaldi
that he wrote for a flock of orphaned girls to play in Venezia,

back when music was first becoming a language
for more than the dance of ivory fingers

and that you staged for the fascists and other American exiles in Rapallo.
We are in your eternal debt, *notre frère,*

as your bones dissolve in the funereal tides of San Michele,
for the little past that remains to us, *notre semblable,*

but we're not playing with trains now nor the barges
groaning with wheat at the Bonneville Locks

with a quarter inch to spare on each side, according to regulations,
and your dear darling Robert Browning is as dead as his *Sordello*,

which we only remember now because you poured the poison into
his ear,
melted his wax to hold up the gold economics

you made of your hand-hammered aesthetics,
in the headwaters of Pennsylvania a.k.a. Yurup, which is one way of
putting it, yawp.

Ezra, stop your after-dinner indigestion and come home to the Klickitat,
the Willamette, the Kootenay, the Blueberry, and the Ashnola.

We are in Plato's cave but the fire is extinquished. It has burnt down
to ashes.
It is the headwaters that are calling, not Dionysus, grey-eyed Athena,

nor lithe Artemis, the huntress. We are old men now. Let's accept it
with dignity,
not literchoor nor skirt-chasing. Bring olive wood.

We cannot wait for you forever. We are beginning to hear the salmon
swim in our veins and spawn in our fingers.

Bring laurel wood and the fine-grained fir of the Valley of Hell,
that hung on a washing line on the edge of the goat meadows

to get the sun in it, then groaned and sang Mozart and Vivaldi,
like grass wrapped around a pocket comb and blown with your life's
breath: *poh*.

Y-e-e-s-s-s, music *was* that simple. It was an *ar-r-r-t* of the people.
Forget the classics—
that was for the tourists. Forget education. Leave your grand tour.

Ezra, the real people need safe passage. In every bar of music, we who are Song
feel the cold flow out of the Rockies, past Golden, Revelstoke, and Needles;

we feel it *shantie*. Bring the almond wood of Tuscano; heave it on.
We taste the night frost, the moon rising on each *le doo,* on each finger.

Take our hands, Ezra, our *leman,* you poor old proud hand-hammered dreamer;
join in the work now—the real work, as Gary put it from his bathhouse—

of saying the name, nx̌ʷəntkʷitkʷ, of moving into this salt-locked earth-ship,
of playing this dulcimer, of coming back, of settling, of keeping what is useful,

selling the rest, and staying in Kalypsó. Brother, come home to our circle;
bring the perry wood that is all that is left of the Garden of Eden,

and burn it, without fussiness. Warm your hands; come home to us;
share a cup of coffee boiled in a blue enamel pot and settled with drops

shaken off the fingertips of the glistening rain that is always falling,
and then watch the star people run like appaloosas across the bluebunch wheatgrass,

high up there above Wishram, until they clamber up the star road,
until they go to milk. Ezra, drink that chert down.

It is with our hands, not with our *tzum,* that we worship,
not with our books but with our *wawa,*

not with your Albigensian literchoor but with our manner of speaking.
The rivers are low that were once *klip,* once deep with runoff,

as eggs lie under gravel and ravens
tear at the red bodies of the last silver people at the end of wisdom.

Let us make peace. Let us *tikegh.* Let us make wholeness;
let us go back to the Clearwater, the Snake, and the Salmon.

Let us go back to the fly and the leader, to the line of the wrist in the cast,
    and the other line,
where the rod pours down through the body into the rock. At Big Eddy,

the light fans, at the head of the current, for what comes down from
    upriver.
Rise to catch the sun's thread and its feathers and the moon's hook.

Leave Walt to his irrigated golf greens. Put down the Zauders
Superior Black Face Make Up, Water Removable, Velvety Smooth.

Use no cold cream. Just put it down. We are not dancing that dance
    no more,
with those process women operating the hot helium-cooled

pile of the experimental fast flux reactor at Hanford. Surely,
you can accept that you are done with roaming. Forget St. Trophime.

Damselflies rise out of rivers and dance blue on the grass heads.
Forget Clais and Blanzac, the round tower sheltered and flanked by poplars.

Forget Chalais and Aubeterre and the white tombstone of Ribérac
dominating the broad plain. The sky has fallen to the earth

and tosses the first word of the world as a sword;
the world is going back to the water; it is cleaving itself asunder.

Do not be in Mareuil and Périgueux tonight; it is 1912 no longer.
We, the land's singers, are walking the star road on the long way home

with the crickets of a July evening above Tuc-el-Nuit,
the burrowing owls of Nk'mip,

and the long memories of the dwarf shrews of Nighthawk.
Breath cannot be denied. *Poh* cannot be forsaken. *Ezra, shantie.*

INVASION SHANTY

If it's about doing something in particular, I'm all for remembering
the wind through the smooth sumacs, and goldfinches

showing up suddenly one March morning, just for an hour.
After sixty years, that hour has not yet ended.

Today, I am reading clouds as they scud
between the pelicans flying north in the aspen moon,

bringing the wind down from the sky to pinegrass.
If you walk among stars, you won't be alone, I promise.

Civilization is over. It's finished. Be a man, or a woman, and admit it.
Now, I know, I know, I know, I know, I know, I know,

to refuse to mourn, to refuse healing, this is called dreaming,
but not by the people who know the significance of each lazuli bunting,

or that every woman has two countries; if you feel she has one,
you have none. Forget poetry. See if it forgets you. It will,

I promise. Its memory walks a brick dormitory at Tk'emlúps
and an orchard's black harvest. Let's not

die there with prime ministers and crickets.
Let's go bouncing over the back roads, in the back of the truck with
 the children,

all of us speaking the words the land taught us,
over the cattle guard to the grass itself, the grass itself; feathering.

Either you know the pain or only praise your own insignificance.
Our selves, we can find in a heartbeat:

that meadowlark, calling from an old fence post
that is one of Maquinna's old cedars, shipped inland and lost to all
    stories until now—

grey and weathered but still standing,
no longer shamed with barbed wire but still calling the sky down,

still doing that old work between the worlds
with a yellow breast and the first sound of the world opening
    opening opening.

WET SEASON SPLASH

All men begin as the *snass,* and only then become the rain.
All men wear the clouds as a *shuht*

and speak as the land and for the land and with the land as their witness,
by gifting away completely cloudfall and wind, and the sea in *wind*

and the wind in rain's blown falling.
Of the journey into the dark coast that only the body sobs,

one thing bears witness to our passing: soon, too, our sisters
will hear our heart pound in the thunder of Shonitku,

when men bare their hearts again, and know
that in the split spine spirit is dancing.

The *snass* that falls to the west of the volcanoes
as licorice and hemlock, into the throats of salmon

and the sleek rivers of their sound lines,
falls to the east as light, in the morning, and holds,

within the air, in the act of its falling, as *chilchil,* buttons,
as Night's cape swings out and we are born as the wind among the stars.

SUGAR CANE FANCY TANSE

As the leaves of the aspens turn to blue stone in Willy's Puddle,
the young men and women of Redstone gather in the dust

of the longest day that the hands are speaking,
striking the moon's taut dog face for a fancy dance that the wrists

are speaking, as the Earth *shanties* itself listening and whimpering
in pleasure that the forearms are flashing, the fancy

dancers reflecting sky and the watchers that the elbows are speaking
out, with their presents of quilts from Walmart

and microwaves and kitchen utensils that the shoulders
are speaking louder, who have driven from the breadth of the Interior

with their eagle feather headdresses that the backbones are dancing,
and their beaded leather slippers and bangles of silver that the chests

are chanting, reflecting dust and drummers and the pickups
that the bellies are speaking, nuzzling

Dodge Rams up to the gunwales in mud, in the parking lot
that the hips are speaking, and folding

bingo tables, unfolded and piled high with fried bread
that the thighs are singing, and just for this day like squalls

of rain children with greasy fingers that the knees are chiming,
chiming just for this day cast away and caught and cast

again in tiny mirrors that the shins are speaking, sewn into the sky-blue
dresses of the dancers that the calves are sashaying, the yellow

and red gowns, the black capes and tasselled leggings
that the ankles are rhyming, of the dancers, their green and soaring

fringes, their bells tied on with red thread that the feet are knitting,
knotted with arthritic fingers, their eagle

feathers that the toes are tying off, dancing the thread
that the soles of the feet are chanting, the thread of the dead

and the thread of the living, the two threads
that are the same thread of the same heart keening.

CASCADIAN SEDUCTION ZONE TANSE

The name of Earthquake's first-ever pry bar: Raven, Raven, Raven, Raven.
Raven breaking open one word: blackness, in every possible iteration.

Earthquake's brushes caressing cymbals in a circular soft-shoe of craw crick,
the shhh-shh cut short by a hand grasping the rim of sound

and taking it in to the bowed body, which is the bawdy of darkness
striking ten thousand miles of beaten beaches shrouded in fog

expressed as the flish-flash of neon and streets beaten by boom boxes.
She is wearing her coat of black feathers. She is crawing their thunder.

In praise of Sand's *salt*, her dancers are all sea wrack and tow logs
knick-knocking to gather at tide line, not storm, not pebble

clicking pebble's raw craw into a rumble of water cracking rock, but a back
eddy bearing the grumbled Pacific's mangled and muddled rum

maw over grizzled meadows of *Ursus arctos horribilis*
and log jams of clear-cuts and decommissioned forest access roads

that are the floor of the Earth, flickered by the lash of the sea,
the black-strung wires' talk stretched on the spruce pole deadmen

lining the high-heel-clicking avenues of Vancouver
with their humming black transformers and bleak insulators for nests.

Fingers intertwine, young bodies of a sudden fitting the find of their bones
and the electric soft touch of the sea's skin that enfolds them

and brings them to their deltas and their tidals, so many
of Raven's people caught in a net of pea gravel at the end of Fraser's
  thin green line,

the children of dreams cooking up Heaven on Earth in a silver
spoon with their backs against a blackened wall of shattered fog,

hammering diesels, dumpsters, sirens, and firehall pigeons flapping as wet
rags being thrown again and again against brick.

These shorn sons and daughters of the cracked
pearl string of brick hotels that lace the capital of all hard scrabble

mills and float camps where Victoria's flag still wraps the heart's fillets
and smoke with steamship whistles and tungsten reflected in gin water

sleep in fits across the purple glass skylights of basement warehouses
as secretaries on their way to *cervecerías*, water taxis, Linux

terminals, and corporate account takeover committees mince
over their bones.
It is here the North Coast *tillicum* of the Union Jack's ha-ha came to parlay

the lead seams of the *pish* lines after the archipelagos were shut
down from Port Simpson to Cape Mudge's dog roses and Knight Inlet's

barefoot daughters in salt braids and flour-sack dresses. It is here
that the women with knives and blood-flowered aprons

camped when the rains came and the bush was spawned out.
It is to these guts that black trains steamed from Canada's dreams of
dominion

over a thin red line. It is here donkeys, punks, and grease monkeys
skidded cedars to slack water, and it is here the *chuck* took each one in

by making a *la push*'s oh and swallowing its wooden *lelang* with a splash.
To these patched streets the lost young of Needles came to discover

their New York and their London and found the circular
terry cloth tables of the Savoy, the Regent, and the Empress.

In these shadows they learned to fight men, not the weather nor horses.
Their city is the silver oxide light of a cold ocean exposing its first

words of brick, asphalt, and Potlatch, the casserole dressed in
Alcan aluminum,
where wealth means to give it all away, every last penny and eyelid,

after wealth became illegal and was replaced with duty,
two-buck crack, five-buck blowjobs, excise taxes, and cellphones

as the people become the street that is becoming the people.
Here the children of Sen'klip and Sea Urchin open a door in a hallway

and find their selves on the other side, staring back from the wallpaper,
with the white eyes of the *stutchun* hunted down to adrenalin

by the jet boats of Chilliwack and Mission: the Cook and the
Chain Man,
the Professor and the Tough Guy, the Prostitute, the Painted Lady,

the Lost Girl, the Wrestler, the Angels, and the Lovers,
the scales that have fallen from the flanks of the lost *salmon*, our
blind mirrors.

The children who are the city undressed are casting off their silk
garters and their rawhide vests embroidered with roses

knotted from beads fashioned where the Ish River's breath
and human breathing mingle, calling them home with the song

that is the one singing that is still ongoing,
back to the headwaters, back to the sand suck and the outwash gravel
    and Raven's crack pipe

of the rain and the night's storm spelling its Morse in clear
over Hammer Lake and Bridge Lake and over Canim and duff
    Dowager Island.

There Earthquake is catching up on watching her children, the *ekkahnam*,
the sea's storied telling; the toll tolled that the pipsqueaks catch

when alone in their telltale cushions with fingers and lips
they whisper Earthquake's name spell, which is too heartstruck

and terrible to mention directly: Raven's discovery of the first mewling
humans, rat-naked, ravishing inside a lipped clamshell,

in that land where anything of curiosity
is what has washed up at high tide on the *nauits*, the breath line's break;

the story of our brothers and sisters singsonging the water,
the story of a man living his now here on an island, *kaaaaaaaaaa,*

that Raven keeps his bleak eye upon, the shores
of which are formed of people, *kaaaaa,* his black eye,

naked people, crawling out of the sea, *kaaa,* his pebble,
the forests of kelp, the old whales singing singing, his coal.

LITTLE ONE RAGA

When I was *pish,* I breathed through a gill.
Before I was mewling, that was my sea.

In those months I could make any face I wanted
I drank the moon's splishsplash till I turned blue. My mother,

my leaf-thin mama mia, was a sweater over a pile of bones
on a grassland hilltop between the Bikini Atoll and Smithers,

British Columbia, dressed in her huffing breath. I tell you,
that woman was my iron lung. I said, *Mama, eat. We are too thin.*

And it rained and the mountains caught the sky on their far faces.
The Ravi and Yamuna, the Satluj, the Beas, and the Chenab

flowed down from the peaked blue roof of the world where my
    people were born,
mixing with the nməlqitkʷ at Acnulox at sunrise

and billowing past the Chief Joseph Smoke Shop at its snuff.
In the bell song of shale clanging its way down to Earth's core,

spring passed, scented with Beurré d'Anjou blossoms, creosote,
and gas clouds of diazinon. Then summer thundered my walls.

Nights, sheet lightning rolled over the ridges. Days, Mama's friends
in the circus tents of their dresses shelled peas, and weaver ants

climbed cherry limbs to the big top of the sky,
up to the source of the Kosi and the Gandak, up into the streams of
    Jammu and Kashmir,

where the songs of my people first thundered at the birth of the world.
The arroyos cleaving from Snowy Mountain in Coyote's *illahie*

were cotton candy spun around a paper cone, over and across,
while I blew bubbles, made fish mouths, and squealed squeaky kisses,

while I was seal and flat soda water. Oh, I was Elvis hanging from a
  rear-view mirror
in those days when I was yet unborn in Washington, British Columbia.

I played mom-to-be like a tabla on the sky's gravel scarp.
I tied prayer flags to her spleen and her liver and hiked down from the
  roof of the world,

down my spine's track through the Punjab, Haryana, and Uttar Pradesh,
slow through Bihar

and West Bengal and into Tripura in Bangladesh and all the ships
of the world being cut to scrap on the mud flats,

until I reached Astoria, on the Columbia Bar,
where the world becomes fog and fog the world

and all the world is the story of the sea,
leaving the land at last, after great journey.

I cried, *Oh, Mama, I whale you. I breathe up a storm.*
I learned what you had to teach me. I fall.

In those months, I could pull back my lips in a tiger's snarl,
mouth words and word rivers of saffron and ashes;

those months, Sailor Dad came into port with blue willow and trinkets;
I traded cinnamon and wild honey from the jungle for his clinker,

but there were no ragas, just elephants plodding in sawdust
and the woman on the trapeze sitting up there shivering.

Mama, we were poisoned by the shadow of B Reactor at Hanford,
where apple trees were left to writhe into grey snags along the nx̌ʷəntkʷitkʷ,

where water was dissolved with plutonium in a concrete beaker
and blew over us, where the grass came to shore in the northern mountains.

We swallowed the poison together and became immune to the taste of war.
Spanworms, rosy apple aphids, codling moths, western flower thrips,

European red mites, rust mites, and McDaniel spider mites
crawled over your face in those days and set us both to coughing.

On that driest shore of the sea, my lips sketched my face with a crayon.
I drew you a cherry tree to climb down to Chopaka.

I saw the slave-taking ants bustle you in and make you their queen,
my beautiful mother with the black wings and the hourglass waist.

I saw trout pour through my plutonium dreams. I saw lips swim in my eyes
like a thousand mouths, each swallowing a star; I saw the moon

listening to ragas on FM radio while the wind blew through your hair
as the sun through cottonwoods because this is your story, not mine,

and you forgot it in order that I could remember how to sing
Two-Spotted Spider Mite, Pearleaf Blister Mite, Pear Psylla, White Apple

Leafhopper, Peach Tree Borer, Little Cherry Fruit Fly, and San Jose Scale.
All these songs set you to coughing.

These were our dead. These were our Bhagavad-Gita.
We carried them to the shore of the night and set them

on the leaves of our words and sent them away to Aldebaran,
sent them away to Buchenwald and Abu Ghraib, to the clear-cuts

of the Monashee Mountains and the electrical fields of The Dalles,
where one impounded river laps at the feet of another, and each year

the first people of the world come to weep for poor drowned Wishram,
where the *pish* leapt between the horse thieves and the wind caught them.

Mama, the dawn hours are grey and I am waking by coughing parathion
in the fields of cheatgrass and wormwood at Omak that, too, are my body.

I drink down the bright Keremeyeus *Liver*, which sings in rapids
        and caddisflies
disguising themselves with tiaras of gravel. I am rainmouth.

I am carrying a message to Rama. Tell him that Krishna is awake,
with the North Star on his forehead,

climbing the peaks to plant a single grass seed
where there is no earth but the moment of rain falling;

I have it on smoke signal from the grass halms themselves
at Barstow, Dulwich, Orient, Goldstake, and Greenwood,

where the first spruce flick their tales and run into the heat of the sun,
that this is the path I must follow, with a fish for a lung

that I must set free, into the freshet.
Tell Vishnu I am a wafer of communion on the Inchelium Highway,

where a people were sold down the river, where land,
without salmon, is sudden and wilderness.

Tell Parshuram this is the message I can get out, past all the censors.
Tell him this is my dream song; I cast it on the waters.

Watch how it is carried under into trout mouth, into salmon jaw,
into stone *egg* and the buried stars of the winter.

Tell him I was born on the seabed; I am being drifted away,
deep into the earth, while all of Bollywood sings in ecstatic chorus

from Richland to Kennewick and Kennewick to Paxçu and from Paxçu
to White Bluffs in the moonlight.

Such a life in isotopes, you would never know we were drowning.
You would never know we were flowing to the sea,

streaming down to Mumbai, to Richmond, Musqueam, and Sea Island,
down to Peenemünde and Rügen, Heiligenhafen and the Skagerak,

down to the Irish Sea, down to Bardsey, Island of Twenty Thousand
Saints and three apple trees in the lee of the green hill, breasting the tide

like a caravel, never still but never moving,
and the seventy-five-cent toll bridge between Hood River and Bingen.

You would never know I breathed Benlate for decades, because I
    showed no *sick.*
I sucked in staggers of Guthion with your blood's milk, *delate,*

but I am no Saudi prince buying emeralds and rubies for a hidden
    klootchman
so he could play cowboy in his desert tent, with his fillies,
    on our wheatgrass,

or breeding *le blau* from one of the three true bloodlines down south of
Empire.
Through the soapstone mask, that my sailor dad carved for me out of
Kobau,

I breathed the exhaust of the Yankee fighters who buzzed my cot *sticks*
and fantasized about SAM missile batteries and the Russkies on the run

among peach blossoms and improvised irrigation schemes first laid down
by Alexander,
but I'm not in the ship-lapped, wind-battered, tinpot-stoved

pickers' shack of history with the bean can. I did inhale argon,
sweetly drifting north up the block-faulted Double Red Spur Type
Red Delicious

ranches of Cashmere and the Agent Orange young kids were spraying
at Winesap one month before shipping out for the spider

holes stretching east to China Beach, with T-bone
steaks and military-issue Coca-Cola chased down with *lum*,

with military-issue rye whiskey and round-assed sand, while being
glassed the whole time
by the starving malarial enemy they called Charlie, who was learning,
I guess,

how to party. *Now* the containment tanks have ruptured. Why, just
last summer,
in the only summer, I walked out into my dreaming, out of the *tule house*
in the Mission,

out into the *tupso*, somewhere where ranchers still shot at It'se-ye-ye—
    and killed him—
before the grass got up and once again started running.

It's not just a story—dead is *mesachie* and life is *kloshe*;
there's not really a lot of *spose*. Not here. I breathed

Churchill's nerve agents that I sprayed on our Spartan *sticks* so kids
would have a *lapome* to take to school for Teach,

shined up all pretty with Johnson floor wax,
but I will never see a sky more still nor air so bromide blue.

The sky will reach down to touch my face. It will have no clarity,
    only colour,
and the horizons will grow incredibly close.

The world will become the span from one tree to the next,
and I will almost see the *chilchil*, then, at ten o'clock

in the morning, the stars. I won't tell anyone about it for years;
why would I admit to such foolishness?

I'm telling you now, Mama, that we are unbuttoned,
but it's no longer news and the causes of the war are still obscure,

although the cascade from the peaks is still *liplip*;
it's still going on. Mama,

I've turned off the country. I've been tuned to ragas on FM radio
    halfway to Smithers,
with one ear on Umatilla. I've been watching the snow fall

on the swollen Earth until the Earth burned in a beaker.
I've caught smoke in a retort and distilled it to a raindrop. I rained it

into the pool of your heart. The big trout in the dark there stirred under
the bridge
that the Green Mountain stages once rode with their click clack at Central.

What the trout said, I remembered. Forget it to me now; forget it
breathlessly:
all the pines are red in Williams Lake now, and all the lakes

between Smithers and Srinagar are drained of trout and this, too,
is your story,
as surely as I die; we can speak that together at last.

Mother, with the same voice you can say, *As surely as I die,*
now I am the face I could not see. Now I am a fish;

I am listening to ragas of shine and smoke.
I am dancing the chakras of muscle and bone. I am climbing

out of my own spine one cell at a time. I am all backbone.
Surely, you have seen that the sea is only the raga of the mirror

broken across the heart's floor? Surely, you are listening
now as her rags weave you? The singers are barefoot; they touch the
sea's body,

and she touches the pedal, and waa waa waaa waa goes the raga of
your earthen
heart's swollen cry.

THE =SQÁX̌A? STEP

The Oregon boys who did the killing did it without remorse
where the trail skitters to water north of Drought,

then went right on improvising rafts out of cottonwood dugouts
and, hiya!, set off, with cattle and horses in the *chuck*, foaming,

their eyes as wide as freshwater clams and their black nostrils blowing.
That was the way north to the Earth's marrow, Fountain,

where sockeye gave themselves to the *tillicum* in the bone game,
with a spray of scales and the sky and the river mingling in *silver*.

Up on the Bridge, men with *whiskey* boiled out of linseed oil and hokum
were hurling their immortal souls into a diet of pan flash,

riffles, pokes, claims, water rights, and difficulties,
and hanging trees from one hilltop in the *illahie* to the other,

back when the world was ending and people were just beginning
to cut themselves from it. That's when Nkwala, the bone dancer,

Hwistesmetxe'qen, Grand Chief of the Okanagans,
Silxwa Yilmixwwem Syilx,

slapped down his royal flush at Tk'emlúps
and called their bluff, the boyos from the sweet pines of Warm Springs

that weave the *wind* and the *sun* together
into a man's breath, his *poh*,

a knotting together of sinew, the clattering of a whitetail
onto its bone feet out of shadow.

He called them cowardly sons of bitches, to put a modern spin
on all the Wawa could trill off his tongue's tickle and swallow:

the ceremonial yack that the land was no place for *Bostons* like that,
as translated by the sons of *les Habitants*

and the Warm Spring's sweet daughters,
who were leading them for the gift of white skin they conferred.

Nobody else could cipher a word of what anyone was jawing about,
lelang their mothers had chewed out of malaria and survival,

yet how else but with scraps stitched together to cover your nakedness
do you talk to a private army of murderers? With salt and a sparrow?

With a pig belly salted in a barrel and a fistful of peas and a biscuit?
To the Bostons, Nkwala's beaverskin stovepipe was aristocratic *and* British,

like a slave in Virginia dressed up for show in a Haitian circus
and every woman south of the Nčí Wána with her throat slit.

Even *les Canadiens* were hopeless at understanding any chinwag at all
appropriate
to the codicils and hums laid down between agapostemon bee and lily.

Hwistesmetxe'qen was. Like the cattle they were raised among,
the gunmen
followed Silxwa Yilmixwwem Syilx and Shiweləan,

as he was known between the silt bluffs and riffles of Snek̓wʔétkʷe ,
the river.
That's what old men can bring after a lifetime of wind in the grass.

It's not much, but when you have nothing to gamble with, you might
    as well
turn to the horses, who came of their own at the beginning of all stories,

when the wheatgrass turned blue as pine smoke in the sun's mouth
and began to tassel and sway. You might as well

get in line and trit-trot across the ice road
and join in as the big dogs taught the real people respect

and a language of wind, alm, and flow.
Although it's not in the law books down in the Birdcages in Victoria,

it's obvious as all get out to every western meadowlark and indigo bunting
that a little lead judiciously placed would have unleashed a fury of killing

in the waterleaf and the death camas as if it were nothing. It is. Nothing.
There is no path that leads home except the one that leads through the
    braids of the water.

A man's calling—this way and back—and all his *wagh,* all his talking,
and his finding his way in through the door left open by rivers,

begins in the *Saghalie,* in the sky,
and falls into the *Keekwuleee,* in all this land down here,

and stays. This is the *siah,* far, the *silver* lifted in *leman*
to the lips then shaken off with scales of starlight.

Forget everything you've heard about Whiteness.
Forget whomsoever has held you in thrall. All men and women

have faces the colour of *stutchun* and *tatoosh,* of milk and the ghost fish.
They are all dressed up all pretty in their dead and smeared with their ashes.

The words all betrayed them, but that was *ahnkuttie,*
that was once-upon-a-time, that was the One Book

with the terrible black woodcuts printed with whale oil
and listing all of their dead fathers and mothers

and all of their couplings and all of their hands whacking the living into
wailing and milk.
With that nightmare buried behind the barn, there is just a path through
the grass

that deer step through slowly. There is just the hills' sashay
that horses were talking about when they were still talking.

There is just the bone dance. I mean, if you are done with the killing.
Reinhart's men have the young bucks down on their knees, right now,

below Mission Hill winery's glass-walled tasting room and bell tower.
Cold water is lapping at the shingle as they pray for mercy, right now,

by making a steeple with their hands as Napoli taught them, *il padre.*
We are all dying with them or raising them up. We are all facing Nkwala,

we are all facing the oldest of all lessons,
we are all riding after Shiwelәan and his horses.

SNASS SHANTY

Death might have us all in her crosshairs,
but I'm holding my head up as I walk into her range.

I am standing barefoot in the water's turning and its turning again
and the wind's unwinding into skeins of tundra swans.

There's no future if men stop bringing the salmon home by offering
    them water:
smoke blown on the breath and caught by the air.

We are one substance. There is always rain's drift
and the sound of the sea knocking on the corrugated

rapids of tin roofs shivering with salmon. There is always this rain.
Everywhere on the plume's shoulder and in its turquoise

knock knock who's there, where the heart is soaked with splatter
is what matters. Even the sun is a raindrop.

Its wind-trembled tear keeps rolling onto the beach at Antlers.
The rain strikes the gloves of bone time

builds around hands of marrow keeping the water water.
We who carry them, it's not that we are blood

walking; it's not that we're not. It's that the rain
is walking through dry grass, rustling.

It bundles itself together into a grouse and flies: a spirit's house; the antlers
we hold before us, this dry grasping brush; these alders;

these drinking fingers; this blooming Labrador tea.
There is no part of the body the rain doesn't reach.

Even today, with barometers, and rain gauges
made of old pork-and-bean tins nailed to fence posts,

there is no place in the mind not soaked with the moment
the sea falls onto bluebunch wheatgrass and hot sand.

Everything is rain. Everything is falling and then rising back up.
The moment of climbing to the Pillar soaks through the skin,

flows down through the bones into the mind's rivers
and pools in the heart's trout, before flowing out

when you dip your arms of blood into the beach at Chinook,
with a herring boat far out, on the rim of the Pacific,

catching rain's daughters. Before there was the roil
of a whale, there was water turning over. There was thought

rising to the surface before descending on a line as stone.
Then there was one word for both at once,

between two windows down which the rain ran.
When I was beginning I traced my fingers along its runnels.

I didn't know what I was doing, but I did it. I still don't. I still do.
There is no place in this willow's net of salmon

that is not the *snass*. It has neither agency nor narrative.
I begin there. Like *snass*, I do not end ever.

WATER KEEPER SHANTY

for Stunx and Puck

Out in the silence Coyote's pups yelp and the hills answer
by whelping more hills, and more hills behind them,

yapping until even the men of the grass lose all understanding,
until they *kilapi wawa*, until they take off their shifts in the bunchgrass,

until they answer that in the *piu*, the stench of dead salmon
pouring off the star road, we are facing the billboards with full body
        shots of a realtor

with hair as golden as Pinot Auxerrois in long-stemmed Waterford
        crystal
two hours north of the yankee doodle billboard at Gallagher,

with its pitchforked cowboy and cowgirl, two models sipping Chardonnay
the colour of wheat straw that smacks of lemon

and breaks on the palate into fresh peaches,
then opening in cool minerality. They are blocking the Chief,

the cliff that held back the ice to make the world when the world was
        a young thing
in the first flush of her making. They are gambling

while Senkulmen's iron hoop dancers rust in the antelope brush,
with a federal prison and a wine village where the water

wells up black from under the cliff face, and rattlers
slip out onto it, hunting. Who are we kidding?

Nowadays, we get our water from a high country
diluted with chlorine, and we drink it from plastic,

but Shiweləan, that old son of a coyote, didn't know about blue box
recycling.
He had honour. He used that. He *knew* the Yakama had drowned in
the dark,

among panicked horses, in flight from Rains's posse,
and Pandosy, *père*, among them, the peacemaker,

the first of all targets, in the ice floes and deadheads of November.
You can't take away knowledge. Know-how belongs to all people.

Only forgetting can be chosen, and with his ivory-bowled pipe,
riding shotgun
on his Russian-Spanish-Siberian filly,

Silxwa Yilmixwwem Syilx was done with all the killing.
Let's be done with it, too. Let's look into our heart's pool

for what swims up from the darkness.
Let's talk to women about what matters: bannock recipes

and putting something into the mouths of our peep-peep-peeping
children,
even dragging them by the scruff of their ying yangs down south for
a decade,

to pick Delicious in Cashmere, anything to keep the little ones
with the mopheads away from schooling's lessons

that all of us—all of us—who love
one child and one woman, one man and one trickle of water through
willows,

where a Swedish woman now serves stout in machined aluminum bottles
among all the empty tables where the dead sit—face Nkwala.

All of us are leading Reinhart's private Halliburton across the
bench lands to Fountain.
What else are we reasonably expected to do apart from burning up
in anger?

The water keepers traded for army surplus muskets used to blow
the buttons off Napoleon and then tossed to Hwistesmetxe'qen as a sop

were no use against the repeating rifles of Oregon's open season.
When the beavers came back, they were blasted

out of the high country by cattlemen and flyfishers, who understood
that it's not land a man owns but water. It flows through the hands,

they got that right, and to some men it is supposed to flow to the sea
so it can become rain and the forest that climbs it.

For the rest of us, there is just a path through the grass, that deer step
through slowly.
There is just hills' sashay that horses were talking about: the bone dance.

Does it matter at all what colour our hides are?
What matters is gathering up the water.

What matters is the dogs and horses that came freely.
Who among us, *s'ama* or Sməlqmix or Secwépemc,

can say that it is not possible to return into the fold of our hands, in prayer?
Who has the right to say we are not all tattooed by the land that has been
our journey?

Don't you, too, have a story of travelling by foot in front of some army
that has lost its way in the desert, until you throw yourself on the mercy
of strangers?

Aren't we all Bettina Wegner, picking up Revolution's flag
from that Berlin canal where Rosa Luxemburg dropped it

when the Freikorps shot her? Aren't we all
sitting in a canoe with the ancestors and Norval, on red ground,

with room for all of us as we come back from the Flood,
the Diaspora, the French Occupation, the Holocaust, the hell pits of Dora,

and the British courts at Lillooet and Spuzzum?
Are we standing with the ancestors of this *illahie*,

or ours, in whatever rock pile or carven pillars
have dressed them down, or not?

Let's ask the hoverfly. Let's ask the rose blossom
swaying in the wind on the mountain.

Let's ask the mountain.
We have words of our own for such things. We have a language,

a *yiem*, a *lelang*, a *Dicht*, a thickening, and a *yil*, a weaving, and if someone
called poetry needlepoint from Sjælland, isn't that part of the glory
that is graffiti?

All true art is criminal. Schütz said that, after he was expelled by the Stasi
from the Republic of Farmers and Workers for not having a diploma

in bridge building from the Technical University of Leipzig.
Love is saying you when I says I and I when you says we,

and falling in a heap together, laughing.
Didn't we beat death at his game, when our mothers

swam the burning canals in Hamburg with us in their wombs
and climbed out, shivering, and ran through the phosphorous rain naked?

What business is it of ours to be afraid now? For God's sake,
weren't you with me at Lascaux, in the torchlight?

When Smohalla came back from the dead to say we *would* be here together,
today, in the *snass,* where wind is the song of a red-winged blackbird

above the roar of the diesels delivering a new load of lawn furniture to Rona,
what were you doing if not listening?

Our souls, the blue herons, fly this way and that above Tim Hortons,
one way with a frog in their beaks and the other with the wind.

After all the Earth has written on us, spirit
isn't the random accumulation of sensory inputs and the noise around
    chattering

synapses of the walk and don't walk signals of Vancouver and Richmond
shifting between wave and individual points of attention.

We have a home on this earth. We are the keepers of water.
Does it matter if we continue in Secwepemctsín or Wawa or Punjabi

or if we dress it up in a sari or in blue jeans and a T-shirt from Hanford?
It is written on the whorls of my thumb and the rivers of my palm

that are the web of the waters. The ghosts of the Swedes at Ballard
are still wrecked and brought home and laid out

and washed by the wives of strangers,
still being received by midwives, and still young women hold them fiercely

and put them to their nipples to suck the milk of the moment. Come on.
Let's do the vikivaki, simply, as they say in Iceland, let's dance with the
dead who aren't,

on the one night of the year when the graves all open wide
out of the floorboards. Let us have some pride, damn it.

Maybe the flowers are wilted, but I am here with my twig broom,
the hazels I gathered from the Earth's navel at Yach

and bound with my will, with the twist of my mind's fingers.
I am the broom as much as the hands that hold it,

the wind in the catkins, that hang all winter,
while the fog sifts through the sky's tent,

where men watch their mind thinking in the scud of clouds
and an eagle catching a thermal, in the heart's tumble. We are who we are,

men and women and children, all of us together together,
all of us being spoken, sung, whispered, mourned, and piled in the grave,

all of us dug up out of a black bud, brought out, and polished on a
shirt pocket,
all of us with five dark seeds that shake out plump into the palm,

where the rivers meet that we use to touch each other,
who are all rivers walking, who are all following Nkwala's sons and
daughters

going back home after long journeys, all smolts in the eelgrass,
and the *salmon* who are the living, living living, living. Who are *really* living,

tumbling back over sx̌ʷəx̌ʷnitkʷ on our way out, leaping back
over it on our way in, right into the alpine fir baskets set out to receive us.

LELANG SHANTY

Fallers in the Ashnola, cougar hunters above the Haystacks, packers at
 Blue River,
where the light collapses and only distance is left of this Earth,

whalers, purse seiners in Steveston, tobacco pickers in South Kelowna,
lean men with wind-dried faces who sprayed dormant oil and lime sulfur

on the Winesap blocks of White Cliffs, black-haired men
who lifted the bones of the Tong dead from Quesnelle Forks and
 packed them

out by horse, teh teh, who loaded them on cutters in Vancouver, trit-trot,
who sat in the hold with them to Shanghai,

opium runners, coopers, glassblowers, *Boston* whalers, whiskey runners,
 and smiths,
among the blue fields of *camass* on the Strait of Juan de Fuca

where as a young man I walked among the stars,
potters in Peachland and Naramata, cougar hunters at Flat Top Mountain,

the Wild West realtors of Winthrop and Wenatchee, the rodeo clowns,
lasso artistes, and placer miners in the shale creeks of Likely and
 the Wallula,

Rock Creek and Umatilla and among the crash
and pipe of cicadas on the Similkameen floodplain,

where I brought my daughters out to the spring constellations,
grocers, Egyptologists, prophets, hardware magnates, punchers,

grizzly guides in the Rainbows, the linemen, political hacks,
and hobos riding the Kettle Valley train,

caging sandwiches from the cookie through the ventilation grill,
the Great Northern brakemen at Brushy Bottom who, too, have shunted

the words this way and that, the circuit court judges and grocers,
gandy dancers and whistle punks, chokemen and grease monkeys,

it is their words we shunt through; it is their stares we endure;
it is their hands that support me, who I am now releasing,

who are now dipping and soaring, soaring and dipping,
out of the tailing ponds at 20 Mile Creek, the cyanide

dust settling in the streets and blue houses, the tinpot
stove and the prickly pears with their yellow silk flowers

in the dryland of an American railroad.
A clinical detachment is not enough. The wisdom

of the hurly-burly of the exchange of ideas in a sanctioned context is
    not enough.
The Portuguese pickers are walking down through the midges of 1969

from the orchards of Osoyoos, dipping their naked bodies
into the dark of the desert lake with its skim of gasoline

catching on its face Cygnus the Swan, Cetus the Whale,
and Capricornus the Goat-Fish. This is a civic sense.

This is an organizational principle. This is the gyroscope of God.
This is the Doukhobor women of Ootischenia running naked
    through their *weght*.

It is the city of Dioce you can still scrape down to through the zinc light,
the rows of ditch-irrigated J.H. Hales at Kettle Falls, that is our Jerusalem.

Sweep poetry aside. Sweep the books of angels aside. Sweep your books
of Provence aside, forget your Great Work,

and sing at last the New York Macs of East Kelowna,
that have been planed down into flooring.

Sing the ash of the Sinlahekin, the Coldstream, and the Similkameen,
where in August tiger moths dip nectar out of delphiniums.

This is not the *mika shantie* of taming a wilderness with Red Haven peaches
to heal the death of Old Man Cotton west of the battlefields,

shipped out on the stage from St. Louis and arriving at last
on the docks at Greata, before the end of the world at Daisy.

This is not Hawkeye, the Indian scout, grower friendly, red as an illusion,
drinking the desert sun at Richland, before the war came back,

never to leave again. It is how if I fill a jug with light and cap it, it isn't there.
Porphyry said that, said Iamblichus,

remembering a man who wrote in the Upper Kingdom,
where the river pours down out of the desert and speaks as an adder,

and that man was remembering other men, who came before him,
and their river, and I am speaking of it to remember mine

and to give you that memory, not romance. Whether you like
  it or not, *mesika*,
you are witness to your passing and to *mitlite*, what stays behind,

which is all you have, which is nothing and everything,
as long lines of motorhomes thread through the valley below,

winding south to camp in the desert with their satellite dishes,
in the hard work of abandoning the earth. Don't be there with them.

Forget Whiteness. Forget Father Charles Pandosy and his *confrères,*
Xavier Richter and Kamiakin, Chief of the Yakamas

in the *Tzum Law* of the generals of the United States Army,
who were in the business of building fences, not taking them down.

Kamiakin wanted nothing of it and chose exile with his sons and his horses.
When he rode across the line drawn in the sand between the *King George* and the *Bostons,*

up through Loomis and Nighthawk, Rich Bar and Okanogan City,
through the wild washes below the centre of the world at Ċuṗáq̓,

past the stamping mill crushing the ancestors to racket at Ellemeham,
he said of Richter, who had fled the Indian wars for the laissez-faire of the British,

there is one *Dutchman* worthy of respect because he gives it. Hardly.
At the heart of each raindrop there is the ash of the Guisachan,

ash of the pear orchards of the Benvoulin,
the best land on Earth for Doyenné du Comice de Chaberton,

paved for Sears and La Senza, ash of the walnut groves of Gellatly Bay,
subdivided, ash of the big firs of Central,

with the whiskey bottles under the junipers and Chukuaskin
and his braves in their graves: now a gravel pit;

ash of the honey locusts shading the Green Mountain Stage
and the cabbage pickers who followed from Nijmegen via Ontario
via Arkansas

after seventy years: now a gravel pit. They still share in thought, *eyeh,*
and so lie inside the world: the four horses standing on a hill in
scratchy snow

at Sugarcane, 9:21 a.m., March 14, 1995,
the snow not *t'kope* but the colour of the sky,

the sky no colour, the horses living in no city, just wind over speargrass
and white noise from the highway, indivisible.

This is my only receipt for four generations on the land.
This is the story I have travelled to on the star road these twenty
thousand years.

This is what I have found in the sweet sap of a Winesap apple in May,
in the bitter skin and the ammonium esters, in the flesh crumbling on
the teeth,

in the thin taste of coffee from a glass thermos,
in the world so thin I can walk through it,

with the bend of a wild onion to the dry ant-rich soil,
where my days flicker and flare: the world and everything in it,

days of wind in the elms and waxwings—honeycomb scarabs scattering
up like rain—
rising from the leaves into a motionless *sun.*

Forget Whiteness. Forget the Skeena, where the *chikamin pish*
were chopped up and canned and labelled and shipped off

to civilization on company ships, a city on piles,
surrounded by dog roses, huckleberries, and the ruins of Kimsquit—

a downtown now called the Great Bear Rainforest,
where the bears are white as ghosts and the wolves eat fish,

rotten or fresh, and swim in salt water and track
scientists through diverted river channels and fifty-year-old clear-cuts,

when there was still a future that was not just the Belgian syndicate,
that ruined our ground—the dry soil smelling of sage—

by selling maps to ivory traders and opium bureaucrats.
We know how the world came to be around us. We know there is a connection

between language, states, and citizens. We know we are of the process,
not learning it: the pine siskin moving over the dry cones

among the pine trees in the evening as owls
hunt around us and the colour blue becomes the world,

the sea suck and tide scrabble, the gull gasp and the choke
of crows in the eelgrass: life on this planet of water;

what it is to have ancestors who crawled out of the sea;
what it is to still be finding landfall, the storm

that blanks out the world while out in the silence
a dog barks and the hills answer with the hills.

HOMECOMING SHANTY

For all the time this land has been open to the sky,
salmon have been rising up the Fraser and up the Chilcotin,

frozen to the inside of the Sun, such tiny salmon shaking off winter's ice,
the soft touch of hands to the body's grass.

I am blessed; the earth that is lost has not been forgotten,
nor the *salmon*, swimming down the long river to salt water,

where I follow: the red-leafed sockeye; the black-tongued coho,
who speak coal and poplar bark. For ten thousand years

of cumulonimbus over the Coquihalla, people have laid their bones back
in its first water. I am dancing by walking,

stepping out like a rain cloud through the mouths it makes of dust,
my mouth, and the tongue in my mouth, and the lips that are the
    curtains of the heart.

Where the pelicans come of a morning summer, dancing,
right now, the Milky Way is a bone with a fish's tail

laid on poplar leaves on a table of snow.
Night closes like the water of Discovery Passage

around the stern of a cruise ship dieseling north to the calving ground
    of glaciers
with its five-piece dinner service and its Nebraskan Black Angus

strip loin and its Brome Lake duck breast with blackcurrant coulis.
Shriven, I stand and sing for them what rain comes now,

slicking up oil in Home Depot parking lots in Nanaimo,
Chemainus, and the rain's own song of West Vancouver,

ringing like tubas as they pour into the mouths of storm drains
    in Ladysmith,
Zeballos, Qualicum Beach, Fanny Bay, and Bowser,

the tongue talk of the black, bitten ocean devouring the white
    petticoated land,
survivor of fires so old its trees are ravens flying,

are ancestor, are rock clack and cloud chatter,
the shape of this cracked song that sticks

in your throat and makes it a craw, craw, craw,
snare cymbals stroked on the floor of the earth.

The black people, the pebble-eyed steeple walkers with mussel
shells for mouths and withered alder twigs for feet,

are playing us playing them, the invisible
brothers, the old sisters, our sweet trouble. At Tofino,

a whale answers their moon with a call in the shape of a whale, and slow
deep furrows of sound cut through salt's blue lattice to Patagonia,

and yelp through forests of bull kelp on the flanks of the Waddington
    massif.
On the Beaufort, the brothers and sisters of men and the redfish,
    the bowheads,

those oaken hulls encrusted with barnacles' bone mouths,
brush the moon with rain-lit finger taps. As music falls in graven star shine

they tralala their summers in black Arctic leads, their lungs glittering
in temples of Bohemian crystal as they sound, remembering

hunters in sealskin boats, floating overhead like clouds
as they lived through the century of slaughter when ships

cast off from Bennett Bay for the body singing the body and the ribs
rising to strike the air hole of the moon's bare bone button.

Long flensing knives and vats for boiling the flanks of *nos sœurs et nos frères*
into machine oil and lamp black were the cargo of novelists in that
    fin de siècle

of the wind that drove rain down off the shale surf of the mountains,
the years when their molten bodies lubricated a stinking sun of factories

boring rifles for the Battle of Shiloh, the stamping mills of the Midlands,
and the black iron newspaper presses of London, Paris, and Berlin

on the hunt to slaughter the Great White Whale of God. We are forever
    its saying:
and the bowheads were lanced off of Nootka

and the blues of the Saint-Laurent were harpooned
in sight of the church spires and wheat fields of the Gaspé,

to the strains of wedding bells and fiddles,
as the calls of the dead lifted skiffs in a black swell in Fulford Harbour

long after they had been cut, flensed, and raked into blubber and rendered
down into empty *salt*, lifting into the sky with spray and the stars' buttons

flaring across empty night in wind and the boiled bones' rattle.
For eight thousand years, the people fished this whales' sea,

where Sky's throat pooled at the first of all stories, the gravel and cough,
floating down flow to Musqueam with the sun, passing through story's
bone fence

with canoes belly-stuffed with salmon, with everyone smelling of *smoke*
and gunwales a bare thumb's knuckle above current

and the perfume of *salmon* riding down with them to rotting
September's *chuck.*
This is the dance that crests the mountains with the fall rains,

the Coldwater, the Ashnola, and the nməlqitkʷ, where the sun is an
egg's eyeball
nestled under stones' knock knock, where the cloud sheets of
the Cathedrals

wash the thin ribbons of tongue's tangle. This is the water that drops
over sx̌ʷəx̌ʷnitkʷ,
where sockeye still muscle through green current with all that they have,

where fry rise from platinum gravel, bearing a single hot coal:
the heart in its continual rejoicing of being here in the green morning,

and still being here in the flush of the evening, and still when the stars come,
drawing close and shivering, and still here when they go.

There is a man who sets down his *books* and wades with a grass-lined creel
into the memory of a man who ties flies to a string and makes of the
death of *pish* a dance,

not for the people but for the *salmon,* denizens of salt's white blood.
That hath the light of the doer; he is all men have left of their homecoming.

He is of the people and drinks these waters; he lives before time
flows from cupped hands into its mouth. Overhead the boats are floating,

that Song is hewing out of its hands as it cups them to its lips,
while Sun's storm surges inland. Fourteen billion years of this universe

comes down to a man making art for a fish rising out of night's tumbled
gravels into day's silk,
the bushtit in the leaf, the root that has climbed a ladder of feathers.

Down with the mergansers, down with the coho smolts,
down with each raindrop that falls to the tidal snick, down into the mouth

that swallows the rain whole, down to the oyster and the limpet's smack
and the cockle, salmon dive and they swallow,

they swallow and dive. They carry the sky down with them;
it bears them back.

Breath is a way of forgetting, and a manner of remembering.
Salmon teach us to tongue it in a fold of a gill:

bright bone comb, crimson rush of arterial blood,
in tremor and doubt. They give themselves up. They flow.

SMOHALLA'S SHANTY

We are all dead men watching the slide rule boys come, followed by
their dust,
pulling up their T-Birds, racing each other upriver to Smohalla's camp,

where Moses trussed him, then beat him, the way you train a horse—
the way a man strips the past from another.

Owhi's people are still staggering, shivering, out of the ice of the
flood river in a blizzard,
those who made it, those not borne south to the funeral islands at
White Bluffs

and washed ashore there, while the boys from Missouri and the Beau Pré
hunted them down like dogs in the *tupso*, in the grass.

Only two hundred men out of forty thousand knew what they were
building with black graphite
and *they* were slugging back whiskey as they drove out, chucking the
bottles into the sagebrush.

The empties flashed briefly, tumbling over and over, catching the Sun,
blinding,
before they landed among the tufted grouse, sagebrush sparrows, and
sweat bees.

They've been there ever since, home to spiders, who like it hot,
and when it's mating season even hotter.

That was an age of the world when boys didn't leave their killing
to machines.
They used slide rules. But I'm not here to tell you

of the poison they made or of our bones shivering
in their sacks of skin. No man can speak to thoughtlessness,

especially not a white-haired man who left the Earth
and never came back with any kind of a name, for all intents and purposes,

among people who believe it is the role of educated men to put people
    into boxes,
to stack them in warehouses—the kind of box in which you can't tell

if a man or woman inside it is alive or dead, or even
the face of the sun written on the rock above the ice cream shop at
    Wishram.

For the love of Spilyáy, why are they even opening that kind of thing?
Why are they looking? Freedom, the Proud Boys call it,

and Moses, who beat Smohalla to the quick, but it is Smohalla,
that old jack salmon who went mad with pain, who died

as a snarl of driftwood and came back as a man at Priest Rapids,
that *chikamin pish* soaking up smoke above a shore fire,

that splayed skin laid over willow withes to dry in the sun,
who is remembered, not as someone who eats

but someone who is eaten, not someone who drinks whiskey
so he can drive even faster, fishtailing

on every sagebrush-bitten corner, throwing dust in the river
below the Wahluke Slope's sweating gunners,

but someone who puts his hands to the water,
cups his face in them, then lifts it to the sky in offering and lets it drink.

The true government of the Earth is the Earth herself:
the blue flame that eats pear wood and the pear wood, kindled.

If this kind of union of spirit and the muscle knotted to the bones of
    the hand
is no longer commonly understood as the point of union

between water, lake, leak, river, stream, pond, freshet, brook, beck,
    beach, drip, and flow,
then each one is a thing in itself, made in some way out of components
    of each other

dissected by a mind given the freedom to contemplate and the privilege
    to direct
all others to play out its drama in dust.

In answer, let us just go down to the shore at Daisy,
where the whitetails wade through the flooded grasses

while geese flow around them in honking flotillas.
Let us step down through the pines at Peach to the underwater orchards,

the roads down there, the bridges, ball fields, and the long cables
strung from deadman to deadman, to carry human voices a great distance,

that have now gone silent, with schools of fish for weather, heavy with
    the lead
washed down from the Trail smelter. Let us be directed by water.

At a certain point, one asks for a sparrow pecking at a discarded apple
on the floor of a sky moving past at great speed,

the hills above the mouth of the Pisquouse glowing in the late season light,
revealing the hill within the hill, both of them seen at once,

which is the body, not a house to sit yourself down in, not shelter
    but windows,
and just enough concrete and planking to hold them in place when
    the wind flows,

bread, water, cheese, perhaps an apple, no books all day,
and then stars, your whole head wide open, scoured clean,

and now whooping cranes flying through,
every wing beat calling a sound from their chests,

whoop, whoop, whoop, whoop, whoop, all in unison,
in a sky of milk, over blue water.

A WHISTLE FOR THE DEAD

When the owl flew across the lake from the esker
at the same moment the sun went down behind the mountain,

I did not think a messenger had come from the land of the dead,
which just goes to show how far away I was from dying back then

and how much closer I am now—just the chirp of a cricket
    calling out for love
in the only word it knows: cheet cheet cheet cheeeeet, that's it.

The dead might live in a land of spirit, but so do the living. We are
    carrying each other.
We are all ants tromping up the firs in the savannah

to cut the silk from caterpillars or rappelling up the big sage,
lugging aphids on our backs, their legs kicking out.

When Kamiakin took in the young priest, Pandosy,
he was hoping for a Clovis point, a ritual weapon

so large and so perfectly shaped it couldn't be used without breaking.
Pandosy was thinking of a God so esoteric,

so put together from night terrors that today the Catholics
have given up trying to explain him and just send the Pope to say he's sorry.

I met the owl again in the winter, when she was so white she flew
out of the air and after passing through my hair

back into the air, so close that the woman I have given my life to
did not see her at all. I do believe it's the dead talking,

although not to the part of me that is living and breathing,
as such delicate matters are put in this country in the sky,

but on this point I'm going to put on my pope's hat. I'm not going to
explain it.
There's a doe that came down today, remembering the rosehips

in snow two years back, that her mother led her to
as the snow fell through the yellow aspens and we turned to ice

as we broke camp and left more than a little of our selves there,
things that we can come back to and visit,

first among the living, and then among the dead,
who are, let's face it, living.

The aspen rises from the earth through hundreds of stems.
The horsetail pulls apart in sections

that every kid in these parts knows how to turn into a whistle with breath,
but to call what?

No, to be called. That's the way it is with the dead. They call,
and with every breath we take from the blue fields of the sky,

or just from the space between trees or from the white fog
the lake makes on fall mornings, we are listening,

and for every breath sounded out with death and bone,
as these are, if you lift them off this page, as I do,

and send them off, among the sparrows,
feeding on the seeds of big sage between late winter storms,

these are the ways of giving silence body and name.
These are the ways a body flies out of air, goes back into it, and remains.

THE MINOTAUR OF SOMBRIO BEACH

for Red Lillard

CATCHING THE BLUES SHANTY

Two years after I intersected his exile from the iron triangle of Alaska,
the mophead was advising me to quit studying books or sitting

in waxed classrooms to receive wisdom
from men who had never gone wild in the mountains,

men who had never come upon a shore and realized the world ended
where the process of their "civilizing"—a transitive verb—began.

By then, he was hunkered down with Robert Graves *and* Norman
    Douglas,
claiming them in the way Terry Glavin, the journalist of this fellowship,

once answered me about the old ones towering above the Fraser
    south of Lillooet.
If you're going to be a writer, write, he began in this chinwag,

with his manner of speaking, turning all his *S*s into sibilants and the surf's
shingle's sussurations, and the wind

in the black cottonwoods of New Aiyansh.
The poor bastard pretty much nearly starved to death

in a basement jammed with ten thousand books
and rolled-up silkscreens of Raven tucked above the furnace ductwork.

He was the voice of the green shore; now no one reads his maps.
He has gone to the *sticks,* to *laha illahie,* Raven's Lair,

as he called it, and the surf suck of the jabble and his shamans, the ouzels,
walking under the water and coming up in the stick game sky plays
with his lineage.

That's what Terry and I were talking about that once,
about the high country above Nkaih and Yawaucht, high above
Spintlum and Tsaukan,

about how a man could see the beginning of the world,
its spume and windlass, to put it to the wheel, up there above Intllpam
and Silicon,

Chilhil, and Seah, above Towinock, Nesikep, Cayoosh Creek,
Pashilqua and Fountain, and above Lillooet,

where Sir Matthew Baillie Begbie hung nk̓yap's people
on the hill above town to bring violence into his own body and to shit it.

Terry and I had both seen into the highest shore of the sea and had both
found we could never go home again; we could only go forward;

we vowed to talk about that, some day, and not too far away, if we
could help it.
Terry went off to hunt truth in Afghanistan; I drove it to the ground
in the DDR,

until it buried me alive and I spoke with a mouth full of dirt,
at Buchenwald, Sonnenstein, and Ohrdruf, where the dead

were stacked up like salmon firs split by hand into rail ties
and stacked beside spur lines at Mission. That's the thing about mazes:

they lead you in, and in, and oh shit. At the middle is a minotaur
and no one tells you what to do with it: kill it, supposedly,

but the minotaur, of course, is your self, a.k.a. yrrr history,
lying in wait like an ant lion on the Cariboo Road

at Two Mile Creek, or that salmon on the wall of the falls at Nicomen.
Five hundred drivers pass it each day yet hardly one sees it,

and some men gone to the trees still call this British Columbia.
They can have it. They are naming a dead place.

Where the real men are going now is Toketic, where the bars
drive the salmon close to the south wall of the Thompson,

where the black stone falls like thunder. Where women are going
        today is Spatsum,
that slips out of the fold of a map like the leaf spine of a stinging nettle

rooted in granite sand in *polallie*. Where they are going together
        is deep upriver,
up to the spawning grounds, where the balsam root still blooms,

and the bitterroot, and the mariposa lily; up to Churn Creek
and Hustalen and Squaam, up to Adams Lake and Switsemalph,

up to the red water of their own blood, the *pish eggs*,
bears, and the cold-bearing gravel of this, the only story,

and from its strophes to the starlight, *tsiltsil halo polaklie*, the white
glinting water where shamans once walked with their bone whistles.

And the fifty Mexicans fishing off the dock at Washougal
at 7:00 p.m., June 19, 2009, with the cottonwood fluff

flowing past on the black water like eagle down, and a young man
with a voice squeezed as thin as a wire out to catch "whatever we can get,"

but without the luck of the Mexicans, who had the "proper gear"
a.k.a. lead cannonballs with brass feet to anchor themselves to the
    mud bottom,

and already a catfish on a line, swimming slowly from side to side,
like a children's toy, waiting for the pan's butter and blues.

LAPRIER SHANTY

I wasn't among the fifteen thousand people who drove to Shonitku in 1940
to throw eagle down on the skerries and kettles

before they drowned under the singsongs of Woody Guthrie, but I am now,
shattered. There is no marker that there were sixteen thousand years of
    story on this water—

the graveyard abandoned above Fort Colvile, with the dead "too many
    to count,"
according to the *fascisti*, for the young folk to dream about for five minutes

while playing Hiawatha, and the swings and merry-go-rounds
waiting for a people who will come no more,

lying empty as their only monument, and the wind sighing through
    the willows
colonizing the bars of the flood shore. "Columbia, roll on!" sang Woody,

who knew less than nothing and thought like a railcar. "This land is
    your land.
This land is my land." That child of plutonium. That cancer.

After all those years on the Ouregon, and the dry creeks that fed it,
I was on my way home. I went to the sand drift and wind spume.

I carried it up in my salt shoes to visit the exiles, Joseph and
    Yellow Wolf and their Dreamers,
in Nespelem, up from the mouth of our water, where Tennyson
    holds watch

like a dream of Samuel Clemens trying to remember the feel of sisal
rope slipping through his fingers in the dark of Shenandoah and
    Ol' Man River.

I left my mouth's sand with the Indian Brand pipe tobacco and
    "The Story of a Cowboy"
wrapped in a bread bag, with the cactuses, coins, mirrors, feathers, and
    tightly wound

bundles of dried sage, there in the Nimíipuu graveyard,
above the Catholic church's blue-painted "You Are My Hands,"

with the toy bears on the gravestones, the *cheetwoots*, the
    needle-and-thread grass,
the plastic flowers, and dried stalks in Mason jars without lids,

and the blue sky with no clouds, the lone elm, and the smashed
    white marble,
left by a university that once cared about such things,

being colonized by orange lichen. More *I* could not do. I had grown weary.
At dawn, I had driven past the T Plant at Hanford. I could drive no further,

the wind picking up the dust and hurling it across the iodine-sprayed
    bunchgrass in anger,
with visibility down to zero and the tumbleweeds

rearing up over the black asphalt hills like a *hiya moosmoos* of mustangs.
This is not automobile country.

I bind it with this thread of water I wrap around this handful of sage
and burn for its smack of smoke, pungent.

Some call it the Nč'í Wána, others the nx̌ʷəntkʷitkʷ.
I just call it the one sky flowing through my fingers.

More I cannot hammer together, with either my voice or my *leman*,
    my hand,
where the wind walks the cloud road, because I am neither the people

nor the lynch mob who hunted them down. I am only a dream caught
    within the *Wawa*.
I am only the green water trying to clear the dust from its throat,

here at the end of time's song singing, where space begins
and the earth retreats from men into spirit. I hope the children will
    come by soon,

walking, to turn me over in their hands, like rain over the Rainbow Range,
when they are that story, when they are pressure-flaked obsidian.

I am watching my books now, swimming with Red's wolves crossing
    Revillagigedo,
the strong pack, as the coins' jangle that spirit riders pay for their passage

from the book people to the keepers of Dixon Entrance.
A boy hears them howl in the starlight. I hear the starlight answer.

"I" spells out a prayer with fingers at the surf line:
wawa kopa Saghalie Tyee, plie, laprier, talapusha.

Forget books. Let children remember us by remembering themselves,
and the weight of them, and the weightlessness that is the act of
    bearing witness.

In our bright time, Voice bore witness in books,
but that was a manner of speaking no sooner tongued than forgotten.

Where the bone talkers are going is not in a *book.*
Where we are going, no books can be written

in the name of the earth that is spilled,
where the rain that falls in the salt marshes of Owikeno.

In the cool *lum* breathing a salmon's gills and a sea trout
leaping after a chironomid in the fire water of the *sun* above a riffle,

then turning back, away from the current,
until one day it does not turn away but allows itself

to be carried down over the polished *stones,*
where the land is the people and the people the *delate wawa,* the promise.

Books failed as keepers of men's souls. They were not rivers.
There was an age of *books,* there was the Great White Whale of God,
    there was *pehpah,*

and there were the gypo camps of Chehalis—that became a wilderness
    of stumps.
There was art in that age, there were Bibles, and there was Tennyson

being cradled by Charles Ives in the Baptist church in Danbury,
    Connecticut,
as he crossed the bar, and there was sunset and evening star,

there was the boundless deep and no sadness of farewell,
and there was meeting the Pilot face to face

where the desert breaks out into the grey whale's chuck, *kah sun klatawa.*
That was art. It had a way and a meaning and a purpose,

and a mud room off the servants' entrance, and it had mirrors,
gas lamps, mahogany door frames, twelve-foot ceilings, and libraries

that smelled of cigar smoke and the *sing kahkwa kalakala*
of the songbirds in the gardens of 8th Street in Astoria

as Flavel's daughters rushed to the windows and saw, in the fashion of
    the times,
nymphs and tapestries and an elegant earth in the ruins of a wilderness.

Where Terry and I are going is more *waum* than all that.
Where we are travelling is artless. It is that day Terry went to the Nemaiah

to write the story of a people who had never ceded their *illahie* to the
    kloshe kopa law
legalized idea of the *tzum* of a place *pensée* called *kanata*

and did not *shantie* for the *King George tillicum,* and begged off
because of the colour of his skin and was told to forget it, to *mahlie;*

the people had no idea what *Boston* and *King George* meant
by the comfort they gained from the idea of cultural appropriation.

Ah, Terry. You left then for Kandahar, with a rifle around your neck.
I drove my grey-eyed daughter to the hanging tree in Dog Creek,

where six sisters swung from the branches. We stood at their gravesite
and watched the lichen splash over the rocks,

with little hearts sewn in the margins of their trade blankets,
that once held down the rim of their last *tule house,*

their home for the summer, the dead tree alive among the flowers.
The lost girls' hearts were drumming,

and my ribs were the sticks in my hand, hidden and revealed, then
    revealed, then hidden,
that conjure men out of the fingers, out of the bones of the *salmon*

cast into the waters where the sky and the earth
mingle on the spine of the land and *tanse, tanse, tanse.*

CASCADIAN REEL

The river cuts through the mountains rising through its flow with a roar.
I stand within it. This is not *hiyu heehee*. This is *halo kumtuks kapswalla*.

This is honest. This is *halo kwash*. This is what Red said,
what he tried to charm out of ten thousand paper hearts

no one had read except him for a century: you have to burn away the earth,
you have to wring your hands out in a freshet;

there is no truth except the work of your hands
that you die of, and the dying is hard,

and that there's nothing for it, all for the little of yourself you can
still find after the books have had their dumb way with you.

For God's sake, brothers, let's not be writing the Scottish play like Red was.
Let's not die at the tail end of a civilization.

Let our fucking books flow out of our hands into the rivers
and follow the rivers back down to the fucking sea,

through the bodies of fucking and dying salmon!
Where we are going there are no monuments.

There is no *man yaka kloshe kopa yaka lapush*, no hypocrites.
When I went to the shack by Cawston Creek

every summer for my education among Quakers,
a Taiwanese rice planter, a Buddhist who had thrown

over a Saskatchewan wheat field for a staghorn sumac,
Québécois *séparatistes*, and a guitar-playing gypsy

and returned to my indoctrination in something people called art,
I had to kill myself again and again and again,

and the bastard was never really dead, was he.
For a few years, though, young men like me were the story of this coast.

A new generation was coming in from work, looking for a hand up,
and Red was there for us, as Mike Yates had been for him,

and our bible was *Esox Nobilior Non Esox Lucius,*
that thin green "A Muscellunge Is Not a Pike,"

which was the furthest extension of Western civilization on this shore,
the story of the not altogether tragic fate of a man who goes bushed;

but then there was the bike crash, and Mike became a prison guard,
a kind of Rimbaud in the Abyssinia of Matsqui,

and Red walked away from the university, because it was not of
his *illahie;*
soon enough I returned to the Quakers, Terry skipped to the
Skeena barricades,

the university went back to drinking itself,
and the stars swung sorrowfully through the branches overhead.

For a while, though, we'd fed civilization our stories and learned,
like Red, that no one who hadn't wandered down from the
North Coast

to Steveston or out of the Interior to Cape Disappointment
wanted to hear about the work men did with their bodies

in a country without maps, and the honour
they found in that, or how you'd look up one day and Pound

would be sitting at your campfire on the Woss,
lifting the coffee pot in the hiss of rain, in the *snass,*

and we'd know they were bushed and would soon be talking to
    tamanhous, to ghosts,
and we would hear them *kilapi wawa,* we'd hear them answer.

After that the place became Canada. There was grief—remember?—
that something as close as the alder-skinned bars of the Skeena
    River at Gitsegukla

should be from a lost world, but it was.
It tasted of used crankcase oil and the cleverness

with which a man ten miles from nowhere could jerry-rig
any chunk of a rusted pile of twisted iron into anything of purpose

and make anything run by cussing it,
which is *delate kloshe wawa,* which is pure poetry.

Red wasn't leading a tribe into the centre of the maze to find
    themselves
and to civilize their wilderness with a ritual axe. He was leading us

in so he'd have a path to follow back out
from Hazelton, Woodcock, Kispiox, and Kitwancool,

where the salmonberries drop their white petals into wind-
    scoured water
and the ancestors are paraded out for tourists from München
    and Münster.

He wanted out of that sense of literchoor and into a moment
when he could be its telling, among his own people, which is to say

in the country of the dead a.k.a. of Hölderlin and Joseph
thundering to the first clouds of the world in their holy madness.

TAMANHOUS SHANTY

The mind stares into its mirror and sees only water: something more
human than human.
There we are, across a campfire's spit and cackle. Baudelaire

is pouring us coffee. Socrates is poking in the ashes for the sprung ribs
of a *pish*.
Everyone here is *kwates*, more than a little despondent in the rain's spittle.

Smoke-faced bastards, we have come to the end of where words can travel,
having gone out to Rilke's bunker with Orpheus, with trees in his ear canal,

all of us giving up our Potlatch paraphernalia to Frank Scott,
Montreal poet, *toh!*, for twenty bucks and a moral sermon,

all of us giving up the all of history that has come down to us
from our own ditch and storm drain,

from our doing and a shovel jammed into history's dung heap.
I mean the Moon, that clear space in the scrabble of each stump farm
and ranch yard.

The word is *bushed*, to go bushed, to lose your place,
to think with the trees and dream with the coho,

to stumble into the desert without water, to go sockeye,
no matter that before Quadra, Cook, and Vancouver there was no
wilderness here,

or to put it another way, wilderness had another name: Quadra,
Cook, and Vancouver,
amidst the foot-signalled laughter and throat-choked greetings of Raven

planing the world with the stone adze of his bill among the
    shamans tonight,
wandering out here with Edward Epp,

that mover of colour, unfurling the land's canvas
as the rain flows through him on its way to the slack tides of Osland.

It's from these slopes north of Tongass that Red wandered down
    from the world
to light this fire. It's here, in these mountains,

where he scratched out a dictionary, on *pehpah*,
so that the words meant something, even for ten minutes,

a yarn men tell and retell away from the cities, which he gave up in the
    '80s as vanity,
in four languages: German, English, *Wawa*, and West Talk.

The first was for poetry, the last two the words of this place,
picked up in logging shows and float camps,

from men who named him Red to welcome him
among their greased pigs and sky pilots and bullshit

and "There's no one in the world the term 'working' applies more
    to than me,"
which is now the white flick of the current's lamprey

at Hasutin as the Weyikespe takes the sun north.
Look, I'm afraid I'm still having trouble with this one word's brace

after forty years of winding my spine on the Earth's spindle.
It's sticking in my throat like a bone from a Yale sockeye: wilderness.

What is it? It's a fine, upstanding mouth clack in a red *King George* jacket—
three syllables, with brass buttons. It sounds like Stromness, with its
single malt,

wind-blasted heather, Royal Navy docks, and darkness, where trawlers
set out
into the north of the North Atlantic to catch the last wild stocks

of unnamed species so they can be saved from the extinction
the ships bring with their net winches and diesels. Red's gone to cancer.

His books have been sold off, body parts scattered after a freeway pileup:
an eye for an eye, a heart for a missed beat. They live on, with luck,

among people who read them, not just with collectors, who shelve books
away from the light and once a year brush off the dust that falls on them

as it does everywhere on this sobbing earth and the ocean that cradles
it and rocks
back and forth across the face of its oldest story, the homeless

boys of Yates Street and their nightly breakdance with the police
and the shelters that are designed to separate them from their darkness:

the light of the mind, you might call it; the balm of the body;
a bowl of tomato soup between fingers bright with grease and the woman

at the brick church in that hour when the graves open teaching them
that candle, grave, and body are all lying their way to morning.

FULL MOON SHANTY

I walk through the Moon tonight. It's just a rock—and yet it floats.
It sails. It streams, swells, is born, and it dies.

It is clawed by Garry oaks, hawthorns, apples, and birches,
the oldest language, the one of two forked sticks,

a man and a woman rubbed together to create fire,
then burning as a black bird flies off laughing

over the crashing surf coming down from Prince of Wales Island.
The air spills, liquid.

Like the poor buggered sockeye of Behm Canal,
I stood inside it when it was a spell,

a stone-ringed web cast by a man in a black hat and his heart in a glass,
which he drank in one gulp in bloody libation.

Like the net-choked chum of Clarence Strait, I reached out and touched
not history but what history is trying to get at:

the mind's sea at midnight, in the way of the salal
and the Oregon grape jelly, the sour sun in the mouth,

the shore pine, the spar tree, and the dead man, that are useful
when you live at a certain distance from Commercial Avenue.

There's something men are that others have been before them
and through them is bound to what they see,

and isn't in books. Don't look for it. You will find poetry.
Quick, spit and cast your breath back over your shoulder! *Toh!*

That stuff was once a young belle's dotage in a dishevelled
mansion on Rockland Avenue after the Confederacy was routed.

Sixteen thousand patriots even went down to Brazil, to raise a new
    Richmond.
They're still there, with their whitewashed churches and crossed flags,

and still call themselves the true Americans. Maybe they are. Maybe it's not
the patriots of Republic or the industrial fruit farmers of Brewster,

with their military bearing and electronic thermometers,
who are the measure of an ongoing revolution. Maybe it's not the salmon

fishermen from the Willamette who came every year in the parking lots
above the ruined docks of Winter Harbour to catch Yakama

fish coming home for $1,000 every five days, accommodation and meals
and an instructional lesson on fish-gutting included,

who are the cast of this play we're living and dancing
from Lodi to Hood River, from White Salmon to Black Sage,

from the Belgo to Horsefly and from Likely
to tide-chuffed Chichagof Island.

PROMISE SONG

There were eagles rising above the Palisades of the Kynoch;
there was Red's conviction that eagles would ride forever on the
  unending wind,

and there was Herakleitos beside him, who, too, carried a pack
heavy with 120 pounds of nitroglycerine up into the tarns of the Itchas,

because no mule was sure enough of foot to deliver them,
and men were, and their dreams.

There was Plato, cursing them both with his silence around the campfire
  in the evening
but thrusting out his blue enamel cup and sharing the bitter cowboy coffee,

if we can give a name to the act of reading the Earth, as Red did,
again and again, brushing the old starlit sands in his breath,

a way of speaking neither of this world nor out of it
that was once our *wawa* and was once the sound

of the surf breaking against the salt hay
around the footings of the sky posts of the big houses at Owikeno,

that I can hear in my mother, and her brother, who picked it up
on their stump farm under the Hudson Bay Glacier.

For a long time I thought you were wrong, Red. I thought eagles
  would no longer
ride the wind, and the wind was no longer unending.

I thought that the land, and all words that defined it, was dying.
I thought that nobody lived there. I was a boy sucking giant rye grass

stuck between my teeth like Huck Finn,
yet it was only the words within me that were talking;

by the time I was old enough to resist words and listen,
you had long ago finished with your basement.

I was restless. I'll admit it. Each spring I left
Victoria's fields of blue *camash* for the red

glasswort and the candle-fingered rabbitbrush. Each fall I came back,
sunburnt, my skull burnt empty and filled with the Earth,

stopped like a mask lifted from the shards of Mycenae.
I walked along the seafront among Emily's sweet peas,

torn smocks and paint smears, absolutely shattered.
A woman I loved then told me it took

me the September and October of each year to become civilized.
Then it was November and it was starting to rain.

My Athena looked into my eyes and saw the Earth there, packed full.
It was the future. Sure, I had parents, a windy house under elms,

goldfinches, scorpions, yarrow, and bull snakes, but they didn't count;
I was raised by trees. Don't get me wrong: it is probably better,

overall, than being raised by mammals, but in Victoria
the oaks lost their terracotta leafmouths and raked the sky

and all the stars crashed into the Strait
where they drowned with a hiss and washed up on Dallas Beach

in a white veil of surf, gorse, and the roll,
suck, and growl of glacial gravels.

Red had come in from a logging show the year before.
For him, Victoria was both victory and defeat.

I went back to the bush, he said, *time and time again,*
until I realized there was nothing there, only a scrap of local colour.

He was wrong about that. He was wrong about so many things,
and right about more of them, but that first day he dragged

a hand-rolled cigarette butt under his cork-booted heel, for an hour,
on the tide swirls of industrial linoleum,

because he'd suddenly realized he needed an ashtray.
It was like watching the devil with his one cloven foot

and the broken chain hanging from his waist, and his switch,
come down from the Tyrol to the rice farmers of the Po Valley,

to confer with Ezra, before he boarded the train to Rome
to harangue the troops once again on Radio Mussolini,

or Hölderlin, whispering intimately to gods
no one could see but him, and declared mad

by the keepers of civilization who had already
declared themselves to be the ones who were sane.

SIX STRING STRUM

I am in the house of the bowheads tonight as the ice melts,
the first time and again,

watching the first salmon swim back to the mountains,
and now leave it, half ghost and half among the living

in my going and coming and coming and going.
I know full well what books are asking me to do,

to become a rag stuffed in my mouth, all camphor,
to be canned on the line and crated off to someone else's story,

in far Canada or Bedford's hidden garden in Devon,
but I do not stand under why anyone would ask this of anyone:

to give up living ancestors and to sell
the Earth for a few beads, a few blankets, an old *musket,*

and a long line of grain barges passing this way and that through the
    Bonneville Locks,
shoving the black water before them or being shoved by it from behind,

and then to have the children of these men's children's children
come to Tsatsisnukwomi and take the beads away,

to set up on their windowsills because the only
language they know for the rain is how it falls on their faces,

not how their faces fall into it and not how it fills them,
not how they fill with it as rivers pour down their cheeks to the sea.

Life is the journey. It is not about the land, yours or mine;
it is about the sea, on this planet of blue water,

and it is not about where we might feel at home
or whatever in the hell we are dreaming.

It is not just for the bee boxes in Russell Square that this song is singing.
Pull up a stump and share this campfire coffee,

with Ez, and David, Terry and Edward and me.
It is not just rain that salmon wish to have flow through men's fingers,

neither in Ahousaht nor in Centralia; neither in Shusharte nor Bones Bay,
it is not rain that will drop from men's lips like bees to a petal,

neither in Galvin nor in Steamboat Slough;
whether under the Flattery cliffs or the basalt mounds of Rialto;

when women sing their stick songs, does it matter
on which stranded tide reach they strum and they *shantie,*

they drum and they toast in their tin cups.
There is only the praise and there is only laughter.

There is only the salt and only the rain and its sea mouths
at Ucluelet, Stackpole, and Altoona.

There is only the salmon and the salmon again,
and a boy's going and our coming, and our coming and going.

Memory is only a song people give to their ancestors
to stop them from slumping into oblivion;

it is only a ghost *shuht* men wear
that the *wind* tears at; it is only the meaning of respect

and the way of honour; it is only what men give away,
and the receiving that is itself a way of giving and so must be repaid doubly

and that once poets denied us, with vehemence,
and the power of legislation and propriety and the buzz saw of industrial
 schooling.

Now there is the waking. Now the wind is a tree.
It is alone in the grasslands, and the *illahie*'s daughters hang there,

turning this way and that way in the *wind* that is all their *poh*, all their
 breath now,
that is all their this way and that.

After all these ropes of sunlight, the grass I am is no longer bound,
either that way or this, this way, and this way again, and this,

because now there is the waking; now there is the trail back down
 to the *chuck*,
down to Stringtown and Hammond, down to Warrenton and McGowan,

and now, past gelding and seine net, past Touchet and White Salmon,
the *chikamin* people are still coming,

with nothing in their hands but their fans of silver,
up to the Wasp and the Ant, up to Kămiăhp and Big Eddy on the
 Kooskooskie.

The rivers' voices are gills. They ask nothing.
There is nothing to ask for that is not already given.

The people who are coming give it to men speaking to the dark,
to the *pish* down there in the big holes, swallowing the *chilchil* whole,

to the *shanties* at the end of the world,
to the souls leaping this year over nine dams in the Columbia's
    cracked larynx,

and from Oroville to sw̓iw̓s, then over the Black Sage weirs in one going,
and breasting the ashen concrete below q'awst'ik̓ʷt after too many years

coming up from the sea at the moment we step down to them,
holding each other within wren call and gull skreek

and crow-cracked kra cackle coughed crackle of what sweet swift
Saaiyouck 6 keeps singing to the sky coming home.

ETERNITY SHANTY

coda

What a long road home. Earth's slavers, with their patio heaters,
cannot be washed clean by the waters of the Assiniboine River,

or the freshets of the Ashnola or the old trails of the Skagit
between the salt hay and the bunchgrass at the rim of the world.

The black water, poisoned and driven under great pressure
into the seams of the Earth to wash her rock clean, can never be caressed

by the hands that dip into a black eddy of the Taseko
or the blue milk of the Chilko to drink the glaciers that were born

before the first quilt of blackness was snapped out over the land.
No detergent and no spin cycle will clean it. Weed whackers

and leaf blowers running on needles of oil can never
be washed clean of the blue smoke they pour into the air or the sterility

they leave behind them. Where there was loam, pill
bugs, and beetles building a new skin for the world,

they keep the wounds raw; their exhaust can only be washed
clean by the lungs of babies, turning them black. No water

first tested on the inside of the wrist and no mother's smile
can clean them. They can only be statistically massaged,

annotated, and studied, with arguments and counter-arguments,
all elegantly framed, with citations and footnotes, charts, tables,

summaries, and official and unofficial recommendations
that are all whitewash. A constitutional democracy

that separates the land and the people
and treats one as prosperity and one as the ritual fountain of legitimate rule

can never be washed clean by the Bow River, the Milk,
the Saskatchewan, or the blue Kleena Kleene

as they rush away from the sea, or towards it,
in the land's buckling and folding and its stark witness to whitewash.

Those writers who prosper by writing stories of heroes
wrestling demons according to plot arcs and proven formulas

for mixing character and action to appeal to animal intelligence
that once released in the bloodstream can never be washed clean

from the gravel of the Atnarko, the Tulameen, or the Bridge River
and can never return to the sky from the sea as the cold silver

people of the rain, each carrying in its mouth a hot coal,
know the pain in the wrist that comes from painting whitewash.

The black cube of B Reactor that brought the Sun to Earth
and blew it up immediately to kill fifty thousand people in a flash

because they would never accept the yoke and the harness
of the 6th Avenue Elevated Line can never be washed clean

of the Wánapam fishers who were turned away at the gates
by military police when they came to pull the songs of their ancestors

from the water, nor of the iodine, caesium,
and plutonium within the sand, with its million black eyes,

that never sleeps, that is always working,
brooding, and breeding whitewash.

The oil pools that dot the oil country, the black crown
of the tar pots in which the green-breasted ducks land

on their way to the oil-soaked snow of the North or the oil-drenched
marshes of the wild state of Texas and the black

robe of the silk wrapped around and around a steel pipe to ease it
into the earth with stirrups, pipe wrenches, and forceps,

can never be washed clean of the soil that seeps out of the 1950s oil furnace
fitted in place of the old cookstove on which my mother, and hers,

once cooked up the angel food cake and ten-minute frosting
that used to wash the cheeks and noses of children white as snow,

before they were scrubbed clean by all the waters of the Earth,
carrying mergansers around all the bends and the eddies

and into the pages of legal a.k.a. corporate
accommodations and moral judgments that are all whitewash.

Forgive me, my rivers, I know you do not flow with milk now,
down over the Earth's breast, through groves of spruce,

brakes of willow, and herds of mule deer. I know you flow with black oil.
I know it is my role as a citizen of the oil state to throw in a match,

to pull up a lawn chair and hold my hands towards them for warmth,
turning them this way and that until they are evenly black;

I know it is my role to scoop the black oil up and splash it over my face,
rubbing it in until all my pores are blackened with whitewash.

I know that Oil wears a war bonnet now.
I know that she is as white as Dolly Parton, Miss Kitty, and Laura Secord

and carries a six gun strapped to her side in rhinestone
holsters like Miss February in *Apocalypse Now*.

I know that every morning she rises from the white sheets of dawn,
stretches her white body, lets her white robe fall to the floor,

steps into the white shower, draws the curtain, and turns on the black oil.
It pours over her with the sweet smell of methane. Every morning,

she lets it run over her face and through her hair
and rubs it with blackened hands over every inch of her body

until she is as black as money itself, then turns the tap off,
steps onto the white mat, dripping with oil,

with oil welling from her opened lips and pouring from her eyes,
bites off a match in her teeth, and goes up like a line of napalm laid
    down at tree line.

Black geese rise from the black lakes of the north and fly into the black
    hole of her mouth
that was once the sun and are gone. Terrible and beautiful,

she rakes the stars from the sky, staining them black with her touch
and casting them down on the white page of the sun,

because she is not looking for us. We are nothing to her.
She is looking for the sun. She is looking to burn.

Even now, her black cloud is rising over the mountains
and blowing west at the speed of the Earth turning among the stars, yet

even now the silver salmon are starting to bone up the black rivers to
their old redds,
where the people are beating drums and singing in the first moments
of the world,

in the terrible wheel of darkness and the bone-white weal of light.
There's more to the world of human relations than human relations.

We are sitting down around the *sun*'s fire with the ancestors, talking
in Earth's tumbled gravels of stars and milt, turning

in great currents over her deep valleys, cut by the chatter
of sandhill cranes flying south with the wind in the starlight,

high up, where the black spruce *sticks*
and *la monti* do not break the endless sky.

GLOSSARY OF CHINOOK WAWA

Chinook Wawa: the language of trade and diplomacy in the Northwest Coast of North America, as developed by the wives of traders at Fort Vancouver on the Columbia River; a blend of Nuu-chah-nulth, Tsinuk, English, Hawaiian, and French. It became universally spoken throughout the Pacific Northwest.

ahnkuttie: *before now, long ago*
book: *book*
Boston: *American*
camass, camash, camas: *camas lily, a staple foodstuff*
canim: *boat, canoe*
canim tillicum: *killer whales*
cayuse: *horse*
cheetwoot: *black bear*
chikamin: *silver, money*
chikamin pish: *sockeye (silver) salmon*
chilchil: *buttons, stars*
Chinook wawa: *this language*
chuck: *lake, sea*
delate: *straight, direct, true*
delate kloshe wawa: *poetry, prayer*
delate wawa: *promise*
Dutchman: *German*
egg: *egg*
ekkahnam: *tale, story*
eyeh: *yes*
glease: *fat, grease*
halo: *none, empty*
halo kumtuks kapswalla: *ignorant assumption*
halo kwash: *fearless, honest*
hiya moosmoos: *stampede*
hiyu heehee: *laugh, joke*
house: *house*
illahie: *land, country*

kahkwa kalakala: *birdsong*
kah sun klatawa: *everywhere under the sun, the world*
kátsuk: *middle, centre*
keekwulie: *low, also applied to a pit house*
kilapi: *to turn, to return*
kilapi wawa: *answer*
King George: *Englishman, English*
kleh: *key*
klip: *deep*
klootchman: *woman*
kloshe: *good*
kloshe kopa law: *lawful*
kwan kwan illahie: *the land of the thunder*
kwates: *sour*
laha illahie: *the salal country*
lapome: *apple*
laprier: *prayer*
la monti: *mountains*
la push: *mouth*
la tahb: *table*
le blau: *European horse*
le doo: *finger*
lelang: *tongue, language*
leman: *hand*
liplip: *to boil*
liver: *river*
lum: *rum*
mahlie: *relax*
man: *man*
man yaka kloshe kopa yaka lapush: *hypocrite*
mesachie: *bad, wicked*
mesika: *us*
mika shantie: *your song*
mitlite: *sit, stay, remain*
moon: *moon*
musket: *musket*
nauits: *offshore, shore, bank, beach*

oolichan: *candlefish, source of* glease
pasiooks: *French Canadian*
pe: *and*
pehpah: *paper*
pish: *fish*
pish eggs: *fish eggs*
pitchah: *narrow*
piu; piu-piu: *smell, stink*
plie: *prayer*
poh: *breath*
polallie: *flour, dust, sand*
saghalie: *high, up, in the sky*
salmon: *salmon*
salt: *salt*
shantie: *song, sing*
shuht: *shirt*
siah: *far*
sick: *sick*
silver: *silver*
silver salmon: *steelhead*
sing kahkwa kalakala: *birdsong*
s'lahal: *the bone game, the stick game; a gambling game*
smoke: *smoke*
snass: *rain (onomatopoeic)*
spose: *if, what if, imagine*
stick: *tree*
stone: *stone*
stutchun: *sturgeon*
sun: *sun*
talapusha: *prayer*
tamanhous: *ghost*
tanse: *dance*
tatoosh: *butter, grease*
teh teh: *to trot*
tikegh: *want, wish, love, like*
tillicum: *people*
t'kope: *white*

toh: *(spitting)*
tsiltsil halo polaklie: *the Milky Way*
tule: *reed*
tule house: *summer house*
tupso: *grass*
tzum: *spots, writing*
Tzum Law: *written law, law book*
wagh: *to pour out, to vomit*
waum: *warm*
wawa: *language*
wawa kopa Saghalie Tyee: *Our Father Who Art in Heaven*
weght: *yes, also, more*
whiskey: *whiskey*
wind: *wind, breath*
yiem: *story*

Cascadia reaches from Northern California to Yukon. Its history is anchored in the mixed-race culture of Canadians in today's Oregon and in Chinook Wawa, the language their Indigenous wives wove from Nuu-chah-nulth, Tsinuk, Hawaiian, French, and English on the lower Columbia River in the 1830s. It has many stories linked closely to place. Here are some.

"Bone Song"
Canim Bay is Canoe Bay on kłúsx̌nítkʷ (Okanagan Lake), part of the *tmxʷulaʔxʷ*, the interwoven "land-and-water" of Syilx culture.

"Saying the Names Shanty"
The poem sings the Okanagan and Similkameen Valleys and Rocky Mountain crossings to Canada, including the Crowsnest (Highway 3), Illecillewaet (in Rogers Pass on Highway 1), the mountain and story called c̓up̓áq̓ (Chopaka), q'awst'itkʷ (Okanagan River), kłlil'xʷ (Spotted Lake), sw̓iw̓s (the Crossing; a point, village, and burial site on Osoyoos Lake), snkx̌ykntn (a creek across from Revelstoke), sqáx̌aʔ and t'wcin (new and old designations for Skaha Lake) and túkʷtúlaʔxʷ (Cathedral Range).

"Song for the Lovers"
Cawston is a farming settlement in the Similkameen. Hrafnseyri is one in Iceland's West Fjords, active in the formation of the tenth-century Icelandic Commonwealth and of the twentieth-century Republic of Iceland. Henri Gaudier-Brzeska (1891–1915) was a sculptor lost to World War I.

"Macadam Shanty"
A weaving of villages and peoples from the wet west of Cascadia to its dry east, from Haida Gwaii and the old trading trails through the Nicola Country to the exiles Thunder Rising (Chief Joseph of the Nimíipuu) and his wife, Springtime.

"Shanty for the Ceremony of Tears"

The poem links five invasions. 1. The Ceremony of Tears, a farewell to salmon before Grand Coulee Dam filled and an invitation to return. 2. The Chilcotin War (1864), for which six chiefs, including Klatsassin, were hung, then fully exonerated in 2018. Tsilhqot'in territory includes Tŝ'ilʔoŝ and the Chezacut. 3. The Manhattan Project, which used the land between four Yakama fish camps, including at the orcharding town of Hanford, to create the bomb. The 300 Area prepared uranium. B Reactor was the plutonium breeder. 4. The Flight of the Nez Perce (Nimíipuu) ended at Havre, Montana, after they outmanoeuvred the US Army for nearly 1,200 miles, including at Big Hole (a failed genocide). 5. The Cayuse War (1848) and the loss of Liksiyu and Yumati'la sovereignty from Pášx̣a (Walla Walla Valley) to Tamalám at the mouth of the Umatilla River to the west and Dixie on the trail to the Cascadian northeast. Roosevelt here is the president and not yet the settlement eventually named after him. Fat Man is the bomb of Columbia River plutonium dropped on Nagasaki.

"Round for the Mind of the World"

Siyaʔ is a Syilx food chief, also known as saskatoon. Vaseux is a lake in the Okanagan Valley.

"Truth and Reconciliation Shanty"

The barefoot man is Father Charles Pandosy, ridiculed at Fort Nez Perce in 1848 for walking barefoot 120 miles from the Kittitas Valley to earn respect from the Yakama. The Keremeyeus River is the fur-trade-era name for the Similkameen Valley's Keremeos Creek. Lucy Simla (Sʔímlaʔxʷ) was the Syilx wife of Frances Xavier Richter, a Bohemian cattleman whose registration of her land helped found industrial British Columbia. The Similkameen Valley's Kobau Mountain (Meadow Head) was probably named by Richter and likely refers to grazing (or plucking or scalping) an eagle's bald head. Note: as a teen, Richter was captured (and probably briefly enslaved) by the Apache; later, Apaches came to the Similkameen to collect eagle feathers. The cleft mentioned defines a hunting trail likely over ten thousand years old.

"Hunger Shanty"

The poem pays a family debt to the Stó:lō. Bruno Leipe (1901–1971) is my grandfather. Cernunnos is a Celtic forest god. Breslau is Wrocław, Poland, my family's ancestral home. Kojoti is the term for the trickster Coyote, which a Secwépemc friend asked me to use to keep the name's pan-cultural stature clear. *Genossin* is an East German term for a female comrade. sx̌ʷəx̌ʷnitkʷ is Okanagan Falls, a Syilx fishery. Baba Yaga is a Russian witch. Väinämöinen is a hero and smith from Iron Age Finland. Black Sage is a shrub steppe (and winery) south of Oliver.

"Wisdom Shanty"

Camas Prairie is a wheat field on a Nimíipuu root-gathering ground. Glyphosate is a weed killer essential to the growing of industrial wheat. Roundup is a trade name for it. Cau'amuitk holds a chert quarry above the Nč'í Wána (Columbia River). The Horse Heaven is wheat land above the Lower Yakima River. In the twentieth century, settlers released their horses there when they bought their first Model T. Their descendants are now critically eroding the unplowed section of the hills in the Yakama Nation. Secwepemctsín is the language of the Secwépemc, taught to me by Janice Frank. The redfish are kokanee, small landlocked sockeye salmon native to several Cascadian lakes.

"Marble Mountain Song"

The Marble Range is an uplifted limestone seabed that unites coastal and Interior weather on the southern edge of the Cariboo Plateau. Its eskers cradle Big Bar Lake and its loons.

"Weightless Shanty"

A poem reaching back to the Mediterranean spices za'atar and sumach, and forward to my years as a young farmer in the Similkameen, the land of the Sməlqmix. Two of their oldest villages are in the Cathedral Lakes and Acnulox, where the nʔaysnúlaʔxʷ (Ashnola) empties into the nməlqitkʷ.

"Shotgun Shanty"

A celebration of a poetic tradition, stretching from years farming at Brushy Bottom and Cawston in the Similkameen Valley, and my passage through snk̓ʼy̓ép's (Kojoti's) stories in the Nlaka'pamux country (including Cook's Ferry, Spahats, and Basque Ranch) to my new home in the Cariboo. The Vernon street poet John La Greca, former gardener to the painter Sveva Caetani, and Lorne Dufour, who horse-logged under the Gibraltar Mine east of McLeese Lake, share this tradition. Fountain (Xaxli'p) is a St'át'imc village above the Fraser River, occupied by American miners who shot their way north up Okanagan and Similkameen Trails in 1858. *Kalook* is "hello" in raven language. Tsq'éscen' is Canim Lake, a Secwépemc village.

"Bella Ciao Shanty"

"Bella Ciao," the Italian partisan ballad of farewell on going to the mountains to fight the Germans, links to Pound hiding in Rapallo from the tragedy of World War I, which enraged him in Kensington, and his arrest by partisans in 1943 for wartime broadcasts on Italian radio. He had stayed for his daughter, a devotion linked here to the hearts of the Syilx and Secwépemc worlds, the falls at sx̌ʷəx̌ʷnitkʷ and the river confluence at Tk'emlúps (Kamloops). Rilke made his own stand in the Valais late in life. The wind that blows over his grave in Raron passes on to Europe's highest vineyards at Visperterminen, the Matterhorn, and the universe, as he put it.

"Beacon Rock Shanty"
Beacon Rock is a lost village site below the inundated Cascade Rapids. The Eel Trail is the Klickitat Canyon, which brought lamprey eels to the Yakama camp among the cinder cones and the Brides of the Sun, an old story that unfolds as you walk the trails between the volcanoes. The orchards of the old villages of Cowiche and Tieton above Yakima and of the Wenatchee area to the north display the instability of settler cultures, as does the ruined Inland Empire of Ritzville and Washtucna, the marginalization of rural 100 Mile House and Squilax, and the dreams of a land-based Indigenous country, shared by French Canadians and Americans in Champoeg in the French Prairie, the *Champs Pays*, the Grassland Country.

"Chilcotin Singalong"
The Tsilhqot'in continue to defend sacred Teẑtan Biny (Fish Lake) against destructive mining proposals. The villages here are from the Chilcotin Plateau and Williams Lake, a region long-crossed by "grease trails" carrying prized fermented oolichan grease. Other struggles are in Xatśūll (Soda Creek), a long-industrialized Secwépemc village north of Williams Lake; Ts'Peten (Gustafson Lake,) which suffered an armed standoff in 1995 over a Sundance and sloppy land law; Splatsin, a Secwépemc village squeezed by colonial logging; Esk'et (Alkali Lake), a Secwépemc village orphaned from its lake by the ranch that preempted it; and Silesia, my ancestral homeland: Polish, then Prussian, then Bohemian, then Austrian, then Prussian, then German, then Polish again.

"Saying It Backwards Shanty"
In 1922, Ezra Pound edited his fellow American T.S. (Tom) Eliot's *The Waste Land* to create modern British verse, a neat trick. This poem turns them on their heads, with Eliot editing Pound in Cascadia, as if he hadn't lost his way in Europe, where he fashioned himself after the Provençal troubadour Bernart de Ventadorn. Erich Honecker headed the Stalinist colony of East

Germany. Chief Owhi's Na-sik-elt Fishery drew four thousand people a year to the Pisquouse (Wenatchee) River, akin to the union of water, land, and voice in Homer's polyphloesboean surf, as Pound noted. So did the regional fishery at Čamná, at the mouth of the Yakima River. Unfortunately, Pound didn't also note that he needed to unite with a place, as the poet W.S. Merwin eventually did in Hawaii. Weyíilet (Place of Waving Grass) was the site of a Pásx̣apa village and the Waiilatpu Mission, which promised spirituality but largely brought only settlers, disease, misunderstanding, murder, and war.

"Salish Sea Shanty"

The Salish Sea lies east of southern Vancouver Island. I wrote this poem while listening to the Cape Mudge horn from my house in Vancouver Island's Willow Point. The poem travels from snow geese overwintering on the Fraser and Skagit estuaries and summering in Yukaghir (Siberia), to villages on Discovery Passage, which carries the Fraser's salmon past Cape Mudge, north and south from the Salish Sea.

"Prodigal Son Shanty"

The poem invites Ezra to come home to do the real work, weaving his interests in Europe with parallel ones in his birthplace, Idaho, all anchored to the Flavel House in Astoria, an echo of Pound's upper-middle-class childhood home in Pennsylvania. Pound's corny American popping of balloons (literchoor, Yurup) is set against the real trickster work of It'se-ye-ye (Kojoti), while Venice is contrasted with Tlingit ceremonial coppers. The real people are humans, distinct from such other people as deer, an elaboration often made on the Plateau. The poem affirms the equality of salmon within this larger community as the trading centre (and fishery) Celilo Falls, the capital of half the continent, faces the Dalles Dam, which drowned it. In reverse, Pound's hero, Walt Whitman, a self-declared voice of the people, is set aside for the people of the Snake, the Columbia, the Salmon and Big Eddy on the Kooskooskie, as well as those of Golden, Revelstoke, and Needles on the Upper Columbia. The poem ends with a walkabout Pound made in Provence in 1912, Wishram (in the Celilo fishery), Tuc-el-Nuit Lake on the HBC Brigade Trail in Oliver, and Nk'mip, where the Syilx are bringing sockeye home to Okanagan Lake.

"Invasion Shanty"
Maquinna was a Nuu-chah-nulth chief during the Spanish period. The giant cedars of his Vancouver Island were largely felled during the heyday of the lumber industry. Some became vineyard posts in the Similkameen; some, perches for meadowlarks. They sing.

"Sugar Cane Fancy Dance"
I wrote this poem after an invitation to a young girl's first fancy dance at the Sugar Cane Father's Day Powwow above Willie's Puddle (Williams Lake). Redstone is a Tsilhqot'in village.

"Cascadian Subduction Zone Tanse"
When coastal canneries that turned wild salmon into commodities and their people into labourers were shut down due to declining fish stocks, many people moved to the remaining cannery in East Vancouver. Vancouver's Downtown Eastside was born. The poem moves between its residential hotels, villages that once filled them, and the rich, mythic worlds of some mentally ill residents today. A deadman is a power pole with a crossbar and a settler name for a Secwépemc river. A ha-ha is a hidden wall on an English country estate, controlling sheep without breaking the illusion of untrammelled views. Ish River country is a term for the Puget Sound that defines it by its rivers and its people. The poem continues this weaving by linking Plateau sites with the coastal ones that create their weather.

"Little One Raga"

The poem remembers a radio station in Williams Lake, which played non-stop ragas for Indian mill workers. It is set within my mother's womb, within a North European ancestral homeland (the Himalayas), within my mother's memories of old British Columbia, within the Similkameen Valley in which she carried me, and within orchard culture in BC and Washington, its pests and terrible poisons (including contamination from Hanford). This mixed legacy brings in other brutalities: Buchenwald, China Beach (a compromised R&R site in the Vietnam War), Abu Ghraib, and Sinixt Inchelium, much of it under the impounded Columbia. Vishnu appears in many guises, among Viking sites (another Himalayan culture). The poem ends in the beetle-killed forests of the 2000s. Umatilla is a US military ammunition dump and the ancient Ímatalam village on the Columbia. Paxçu is the ford on the Columbia above the mouth of the Yakima River that became Pasco, an industrial and railroad town that housed the Hanford Nuclear Reservation's Black employees. The Green Mountain stagecoach to the Okanagan Valley passed through the Sməlqmix village at Central (the second of three towns known as Keremeos). I spent years as a boy watching big trout slip out into the green water from under its hand-axed bridge footings.

"The =Sqáx̌aʔ Step"

In 1858, a group of Americans riding (on *s-n-kł-c'aʔ-sqáx̌aʔ*, horses) with the New Yorker Herman Reinhart from The Dalles to the Bridge River gold fields began a genocidal massacre at the western end of the Okanagan Lake Bridge in Tsinstikeptum, while lashing together stolen Syilx canoes to raft their wagons across the narrows. Six Catholic Syilx men, baptized by Father Giovanni Nobili, were shot while praying for Christian mercy. At Tk'emlúps, Silxwa Yilmixwwem Syilx—the Grand Chief known to the fur trade as Nkwala (after his French baptismal name Nicholas), and known in the south, near Spokane, as Hwistesmetxe'qen (Walking

Grizzling Bear) and to the Secwépemc as Shiwelǝan—demanded the surrender of the murderer. To ensure peace across the border that divided his territory, he led the Americans to the gold fields, dressed symbolically in a top hat, possibly as a lesson in respect drawn from the old story of Dog and Horse, who alone helped the ignorant and helpless. Drought is south of Tsinstikeptum. The bone game is s'lahal, a spiritual gambling game played in Cascadia twelve thousand years ago (with mammoth bones) and still played today. In his own efforts at peace, British Columbia's founding magistrate, Sir Matthew Baillie Begbie, designated hanging trees in major Indigenous settlements in the Fraser drainage. Warm Springs is the reserve that housed the Liksiyu (Cayuse) after they were dispossessed in 1848. It sheltered many Canadian mixed-race families after the racialization of Oregon. The Haitian circus is the 1791 Haitian Revolution, which terrified men trying to set up slave states in Cascadia to stave off civil war in the South. The Birdcages was the colonial parliament in Victoria.

"Snass Shanty"

Antlers is the alluvial mouth of Deep Creek, where English aristocrats camped for a decade, drinking their inheritance in whiskey and roasting overwintering mule deer. The Pillar is one of the Earth's bones, a glacial remnant on the trail between Syilx territory in Falkland and Secwépemc territory in Neskonlith. Its surrounding glacial sediments have washed downstream. You can walk on them today in Chinook, at the mouth of the Columbia.

"Water Keeper Shanty"

Beaver (*Stunx* in Nsyilxcǝn) is the water keeper, who weaves water and land together. The poem honours sites around nʕaylintn (the Chief), a bluff above Vaseux, and Father Pandosy, who became the main target of Gabriel Rains's vigilante army after Pandosy tried to prevent the Yakima War. The orcharding town of Cashmere is just one of the grasslands transformed by the industrialization of Stunx's water. The tragedy sweeps up villages in the Fraser Canyon War and twentieth-century German revolutionaries. It is healed by the entrance of a canoe of refugees from Ojibwe history, repopulating the world in the art of Norval Morrisseau. Dora is the camp where forced labourers built the Third Reich's V-2 rockets under brutal conditions. It contrasts the natural power of *Dicht*, the thickening of water into a drop that is German poetry, and *yil*, the Syilx principle of weaving all things together. *s'ama* is N̓syilxčn̓ for a white person. Stefan Schütz is an East German dissident. Smohalla was a Wánapam prophet, who died and was reborn after being ritually beaten by Sinkiuse Chief Sulktalthscosum (Moses) for refusing to bargain with the USA. He started the Dreamers, a prophetic movement of tradition and rebirth. Yach (Oak) is a Celtic sacrifice site in the Black Forest. The vikivaki is a dance with the dead from Iceland, used by novelist Gunnar Gunnarsson to symbolize Iceland's national rebirth in the 1930s.

"Lelang Shanty"
Cascadian English comes from folk sources, including railroad workers (gandy dancers) and lumber workers (whistle punks, chokemen, and grease monkeys). The Rainbows are mountains in the Chilcotin. Ootischenia was a passivist Doukhobor colony in Sinixt territory. J.H. Hales and Red Havens are peaches. Hawkeye is the Delicious apple. The Sinlahekin Valley is an old channel of the Similkameen. Greata and Daisy are lost orchard plantations. The third-century Syrian Iamblichus codified the work of Porphyry on the mystery religions of the prehistoric Middle East and Egypt. Kamiakin was chief of the Yakama; he kept Pandosy for prestige and as a translator and mediator. Place names are from the Similkameen, the Okanagan, and the North Coast. The Belgian Orchard Syndicate laundered Belgian Congo rubber money by starting Okanagan orcharding culture as the real estate enterprise it remains today.

"Homecoming Shanty"

From the bones of salmon laid in rivers, salmon are born again. A 2009 trip up the Columbia to my birth waters was the same homecoming. The towns named line the Salish Sea, up the Fraser to the Coldwater, and up the Nč'í Wána until it becomes the nx̌ʷəntkʷitkʷ and then home to the q'awsitkʷ and the nməlqitkʷ (the Similkameen River). I returned to Vancouver Island only long enough to pack.

"Smohalla's Shanty"

Scenes from the Hanford Nuclear Reservation. Nuclear engineers raced from there to swim in the pools below p'mná, Smohalla's village at Priest Rapids, where Chief Owhi helped Pandosy escape Rains's posse in 1855. (Rains went on to invent the land mine for the Confederates.) Spilyáy is Kojoti. The Wahluke Slope provided artillery and rocket cover for the Hanford Site's reactors. Long out of bounds, the slope is now a premium wine appellation. Daisy and Peach are drowned orchard towns. The Pisquouse is today's Wenatchee River.

"Catching the Blues Shanty"

The poet and historian Charles "Red" Lillard learned poetry in logging (gypo) camps in Alaska, immersed in two lost languages, logging jargon (West Talk) and Wawa. He landed on Sombrio Beach, west of Victoria. For years he dreamed of writing a dictionary, championed a Northwest Renaissance, and then died young. His poem "Rivers Were Promises" is a dirge for the industrialization of Central British Columbia's rivers to produce power for the Alcan smelter in Kitimat. New Aiyansh (Gitlax̱t'aamiks) is the capital of the Gitxskan Nation, the formation of which the reporter Terry Glavin witnessed. The names here are in St'at'imc, Nlaka'pamux, and Secwépemc country. nk̓yap is Kojoti. The DDR is the Deutsche Demokratische Republik (East Germany). Terry edited, annotated, and published Red's work on Wawa and West Talk. Nicomen is a Nlaka'pamux village. Washougal is a town on the tidal Columbia.

"Laprier Shanty"

Fort Colvile is a Canadian mixed-race settlement near Shonitku. The *fascisti* is a term drawn from Yakima poet Jim Bodeen's remarks that the "fascists" (industrial fruit farmers) can't even organize the picking of their own apples. The Ouregon (Oolichan) is a grease trade name for the Fraser. In every regional language, the river was named after this trade. Due to cartographic bungling, Oregon got the name and the wrong river (the Columbia), while the Ouregon (the Fraser) remained wild. Joseph and the warrior Yellow Wolf were exiled to Nespelem after the Nez Perce War. The T Plant is where the Hanford Nuclear Reservation's irradiated uranium was dissolved to extract its plutonium. The acid baths were then poured into steel tanks. They are leaking. Revillagigedo, Dixon Entrance, and Owikeno are from Lillard's North. Chehalis is from his boyhood in the clear-cuts of southern Washington. Nemaiah is in Tšilqot'in country. Dog Creek is a Secwépemc village south of Esk'et. A sky pilot is West Talk for "priest."

"Cascadian Reel"

The poem aligns Terry's, Red's, and my mother's North with the death of salmon fishing at Steveston (on the Fraser), and Cape Disappointment (on the Columbia). The German tourists here appear less engaged with Indigenous cultures and their own poet Hölderlin than Red was, who read his country in that poet who went mad uniting the ancients and the moderns. Woss is a lake and lumber region on Vancouver Island. Mike Yates is the poet J. Michael Yates, who championed unofficial languages and then set poetry aside to become a prison guard at the Matsqui Institution.

"Tahmanhous Shanty"

The North Coast painter Edward Epp is welcomed to the fellowship. Frank Scott is the poet who betrayed language, the land, and her people by sending the land's children to residential schools. Yale was the centre of the Fraser River War. Yates Street is in Victoria. Has-Hu-Tin (Asotin) was a main Nimíipuu settlement on the Wey̓ikespe (the Snake River).

"Full Moon Shanty"

Red chose exile from Alaska's Prince of Wales Island, Behm Canal, and Clarence Strait among the Garry oaks in Victoria, just as James Douglas did when Fort Vancouver was transferred to the USA, and just as wealthy Confederate widows did, selling their plantations to build mansions on Rockland Avenue after the US Civil War. An industrial Granny Smith orchard in Brewster occupies the site of the North West Company's Fort Okanogan at t̓kuya'tum. The Columbia Reservation to the west was annulled to assist with the business interests of six cattlemen-miners in Oroville, south of sw̓iw̓s. The Colville Reservation to the east was halved thereafter. Its main town is Republic, formerly the village of kti'i'pus (Lone Tree on the Flat). The Willamette Valley was the goal of the Oregon Trail and cradled French Prairie. Winter Harbour is a remote village on Vancouver Island. The Belgo is the Belgian Orchard Company lands in Kelowna. The other names span Cascadia.

"Promise Song"

This poem charts my journeys between exile and home, until the conflict was reconciled in Canim Bay, in my fifties. The eagles of the Kynoch circle in one of Red's poems about the Chilcotin and his own exile. The ghosts here share Red's habit of talking to the writers of the books he had brought along for the season. Place names here range from northern Vancouver Island to the

Columbia Gorge, from the Chilcotin to the Okanagan Valley, and from the Cariboo to Russian Alaska. The salmon come home to them all, or might again. Emily is Emily Carr. The sweet peas have naturalized on her beloved Dallas Beach.

"Six String Strum"

My song to welcome the salmon home, facing down Woody Guthrie's farewell (written for the Bonneville Power Administration and damning the Columbia for grocery money). Tsatsisnukwomi is a Da'naxda'xw Awa'etlala village in the Broughton Archipelago, restored from old stories and a prophecy. Ahousaht is a Nuu-chah-nulth village, once at the heart of anti-logging protests. David is David McCloskey, Cascadia's cartographer. The Duke of Bedford installed a garden that replicated the British Empire in Devon, after constructing London's Russell Square. Other sites are from clear-cut Washington and the lower Columbia (cleared of salmon). They lead to the Kooskooskie, where Nimíipuu salmon are being brought home today. Saaiyouck 6 is in Phillips Arm, in the Kwiakah First Nation. q'awst'ik̓ʷt is Skaha Lake, footed now by the Okanagan Falls Dam, that cuts sx̌ʷəx̌ʷnitkʷ in two.

"Eternity Shanty"

A song that sees salmon rivers, salmon people, their pasts, and their futures in jeopardy to oil. Rumours from the 1930s had it that Manhattan's scrapped 6th Avenue Elevated Railway was sold to Japan as scrap, where it was reforged as the Japanese World War II fleet and began the war that led to the plutonium plants; these were passed on by Pound's friend, the poet William Carlos Williams. They remain fake news but no less powerful for that.

ACKNOWLEDGEMENTS

Parts of this song cycle have won second prize in the CBC Literary Prize in 2007 and 2017. "Song for the Lovers" has appeared in the chapbook *Why We Write*, a commemoration of the screening of the film by the same name. This work was generously supported by the Canada Council for the Arts and the British Columbia Arts Council.

The maps on pages viii and ix were adapted by Trista Bassett and Harold Rhenisch with written permission from David McCloskey from the more extensive "Map of Cascadia" (2015), Cascadia.Institute.org. The second edition of David McCloskey's large full-colour map, "Cascadia: A Great Green Land" (2023), is available from FeatheredStarProductions.com.

Harold Rhenisch has published 33 books of poetry, fiction, memoir, translation, criticism, and nonfiction since 1981. He has twice won both the CBC Prize and the Malahat Review Long Poem Prize and received the George Ryga Prize for Social Responsibility in Literature.

ᐅᐢᑲᓇ

OSKANA POETRY & POETICS

BOOK SERIES

Publishing new and established authors, Oskana Poetry & Poetics offers both contemporary poetry at its best and probing discussions of poetry's cultural role.

PREVIOUS BOOKS IN THE SERIES:

Measures of Astonishment: Poets on Poetry, presented by the League of Canadian Poets (2016)

The Long Walk, by Jan Zwicky (2016)

Cloud Physics, by Karen Enns (2017)

The House of Charlemagne, by Tim Lilburn (2018)

Blackbird Song, by Randy Lundy (2018)

Forty-One Pages: On Poetry, Language and Wilderness, by John Steffler (2019)

Live Ones, by Sadie McCarney (2019)

Field Notes for the Self, by Randy Lundy (2020)

Burden, by Douglas Burnet Smith (2020)

Red Obsidian, by Stephan Torre (2021)

Pitchblende, by Elise Marcella Godfrey (2021)

Shifting Baseline Syndrome, by Aaron Kreuter (2022)

Synaptic, by Alison Calder (2022)

The History Forest, by Michael Trussler (2022)

Dislocations, by Karen Enns (2023)

Wrack Line, by M.W. Jaeggle (2023)

Into the Continent, by Emily McGiffin (2024)